THE *Secrets of* Exactly How To
FOR SALE BY OWNER

THE *Secrets of* Exactly How To
FOR SALE BY OWNER

Juli Doty

100 Malaga Highway
Wenatchee, WA 98807-4706
(509) 662-7600
juli@julidoty.com

www.julidoty.com

No part of this publication may be reproduced, stored in a retrieval system or transmitted in any form or by any means, electronic, mechanical, photocopying, recording, scanning or otherwise, except as permitted under Section 107 or 108 of the 1976 United states Copyright Act, without the prior written permission of the Publisher. Requests to the Publisher for permission should be addressed to the Permissions Department, Business Details, PO Box 4706, Wenatchee, WA 98807.

Limit of Liability / Disclaimer of Warranty: While the publisher and author have used their best efforts in preparing this book, they make no representation or warranties with respect to the accuracy or completeness of the contents of this book and specifically disclaim any implied warranties of merchantability or fitness for a particular purpose. No warranty may be created or extended by sales representative or written sales materials. The advice and strategies contained herein may not be suitable for your situation. You should consult with a professional where appropriate. Neither the publisher nor author shall be liable for any loss of profit or any other damages, including but not limited to special, incidental, consequential or other damages.

THE *Secrets of* EXACTLY HOW TO **FSBO** tell you exactly how and when to sell your home <u>without</u> a real estate agent.

You want maximum profit and minimum hassle. You do not want to mess it up. You've heard of, or survived, agent horrors. Do you hire an agent or sell the house on your own? You deserve to keep the appreciation you earned. Agents will argue against selling your home on your own. They say:

➢ You need to be in the multiple listings.
➢ You will be your own worst salesman.
➢ Your home may need serious help before you put it on the market.
➢ What about disclosures, forms, negotiation, paperwork and closing?

Here is some *Real Estate, Real Advice*

➢ When you do not want to deal with agents....
➢ You absolutely do not want to pay a commission.....
➢ And you are determined to bring success and professionalism to your home sale.
➢ That is the time you need…

FSBO, PRONOUNCED FizzBo: a person selling their own real estate without the services of a licensed real estate broker.

EXACTLY HOW TO **INDEX**

EXACTLY HOW TO INDEX

Real Estate, Real Advice
Exactly How To

Real Estate

Facts

1

Real Estate Basics
To List, or Not To List

REAL ESTATE BASICS

HOME IS SECURITY, SAFETY, SHELTER AND WEALTH!

Real estate lines the road you take through life that can bring you to your dreams. The plan is simple. Buy your next home in a neighborhood where values are going up. Select the home with the view, with the big lot. Buy the worst house on the block – it has the farthest to go up in value!

Are you handy? Travels up the road to success will be even faster for those willing to do some work. A great way to learn skills you don't already have is to hire a project done the first time. Stay and help. Watch closely. Learn. Next time do the job yourself and make more money.

Your road to a profitable future is to create a **"Gotta Have It Home."**

> Your home may be the most valuable asset you ever own.
>
> Build an amazing future by learning exactly how to sell your own real estate without an agent.

SHOULD YOU SELL YOUR HOUSE?

If the first answer that entered your head was "YES, for the money"… "for a better neighborhood"…. "I need a smaller house" … "we got transferred"… "my family needs a bigger, better house" or "retirement", then yes, you probably should sell your house.

If your answer was "I don't know"… you have just discovered your motivation to sell may not be strong enough to go through all the work and stress. Selling a home is work and stress whether you hire an agent or do it yourself.

The Secrets of Exactly How to FSBO is your tool to knowing exactly how to accomplish a top dollar sale without paying a commission. Some of you will read this book and decide you want to hire an agent. That's great. Not only will you have someone to share the work load, you will know the *"Secrets of Exactly How"* your agent should do their job.

SELL FIRST OR BUY FIRST?

Here is the bottom line. You offer your house for sale and shop for a new home at the same time. It is hard. You will be under pressure to sell your home at top dollar. You must pack, clean, stage and keep it perfect at all times. I know how hard it is, I've done it. More than once! But it's worth it when you go to the bank or better yet reinvest those dollars in more wealth earning real estate. The answer to whether you should sell first or buy first is in the following questions:

➢ How many people your move will affect?

➢ How clean will the kids keep their rooms?

➢ Will you keep your home *presentation perfect*?

➢ Would you rather accept a lower price than keep the house perfect for showing?

➢ Can you afford a bridge loan that will finance the new home before you sell the old one?

Do your work, school and sleep schedules allow buyers reasonable access?

> Will weather affect your selling price?

> Are you moving near or far?

SELL VACANT OR OCCUPIED?

Are you capable of keeping your home absolutely perfect 100% of the time during the showing and closing periods? Is your furniture and décor appealing to everyone? Do people walk into your home and say, "Wow, this is great!"?

Then your home will probably sell better occupied.

Vacant is frequently better because the home will not be tainted by your daily life. Old furniture, dirty socks, dirty dishes and yesterday's fried onions all work against you.

Most potential buyers are not good at imagining their furniture, their life and their family in **_your home_**. Unless your house is likely to constitute a move up and your décor reinforces the lifestyle improvement, your belongings may make the visualization process even more difficult. It can be much easier for a buyer when your family and personality are gone.

If you can not afford to move before you sell, then read and follow the directions in Chapter 4, "Setting the Stage." You will do great!

WAIT!
SHOULD YOU SELL THE HOUSE, OR RENT IT OUT?

Rental real estate is the foundation of many fortunes. Your tenant essentially purchases real estate for you. You earn extra income and tax reduction at the same time. In the future, the rental real estate will be paid off and you can sell it for a windfall of cash.

An experienced landlord will sell when the tax benefits have reached a low point, but use a 1031 exchange to defer any taxes into the future.

Do you have the personality and skills to be a landlord?

➢ Can-Do Attitude

➢ Ability to maintain and repair the house as needed

➢ Ability to deal in a positive manner with people of many personalities

➢ Willingness to keep simple books and use tax benefits

➢ Desire to improve your life's potential

If you are in a good rental market and can afford to buy without selling, consider becoming a landlord. The income from your rental should pay the current mortgage, taxes, insurance and repairs.

TO LIST OR NOT TO LIST?

That is the question. Selling your home is a critical, time sensitive job. Some home owners do a great job. Others do not. Decide whether or not YOU should be your own agent before you put your home on the market.

HOME OWNERS SAY, "Why pay a real estate agent?"

➢ I can sell it myself and end up with more money.

➢ If I sell it myself then I keep control.

➢ No one knows the house like I do.

➢ I can handle the forms. I do paperwork all day at the office.

➢ Real estate agents don't do anything, They never even call you back.

REAL ESTATE AGENTS SAY, "You need professional help!"

➢ Listed homes sell for 9%-15% higher than FSBOs.

➢ 70% of FSBO homes give up and list with an agent.

➢ Home owners run off buyers.

➢ Home owners don't understand the rules.

➢ The work load is tremendous, home owners never really understand what is involved in selling their home until they have messed it up!

WHO IS RIGHT?

Make sure you are.

YOUR GOALS ARE

➤ Sell for top dollar

➤ Sell when you need to sell

➤ Enjoy a no hassle transaction

Knowing exactly how to sell your home for top dollar, allows you to make a decision on whether you want a professional real estate agent to do the work or if you have the time and ability to do this yourself.

No matter which method you choose, you must understand a real estate agent's job well enough to know which agents do a good job and exactly what must be done through the sales process. You deserve the best from your agent, even if that agent is you.

Who can you trust with the listing, negotiation, preparation and legalities of selling your home? A bad choice places you at risk for disclosure problems, lawsuits and may cost much more than a real estate commission.

The real estate profession frequently attracts people who need part-time flexible hours and love looking at homes. They have no idea how demanding the job will become.

Many have no idea they have power over your largest asset. Real estate also attracts opportunists. It is your job to honestly assess whether your best answer is to list with an excellent real estate agent or sell by owner.

REAL ESTATE AGENTS

What does a comparison of these two professional licensing requirements from the 2007 Washington State Department of Licensing regulations tell you?

Real Estate License Requirements	Cosmetologist License Requirements
60 Hours	**1600 hours**
➤ Be 18 years of ➤ Complete a **60** clock hour course in real estate fundamentals ➤ Pass the WA State Dept of Licensing exam	➤ Be at least 17 years of agent ➤ Graduate from a school approved and licensed by the WA Dept of Licensing with a minimum of **1600** required state hours

If you decide to hire a real estate agent, hire expertise and a top notch reputation, not just a license!

A LISTING AGENT is contracted to honestly work to get the highest price and best terms possible for the seller. The listing agent must tell the buyer's secrets to the seller.

A BUYER AGENT is contracted with the buyer to honestly work to get the best terms and lowest price for the buyer. The buyer agent must tell the buyer any secrets of the seller they can discover. A buyer agent should verify pricing on all properties they write up.

A DUAL AGENT is, within the law, attempting to work fairly for both buyer and seller. Dual agency is sometimes the best bet and often the worst bet, for the seller and buyer. A dual agent is charged to be fair to everyone. I personally do not know how a dual agent can be fair to all parties according to the above criteria. At times, dual agency is a reasonable solution when everyone is willing to bend.

Dual agency is also a tempting way for the agent to place their personal priorities ahead of the seller or buyer.

Consider the following situation. A buyer calls the listing agent to see a $400,000 house. The buyer likes it, but wants to see everything in their price range. At the end of all these showings, the buyer tells the agent to go ahead and write an offer at $350,000 on the agents own listing, the very first house the buyer saw.

The listing agent, who has also been acting as their buyer agent, has just that day received an offer from an outside buyer agent at $370,000.

The dual agent (now working for both seller and buyer) has a serious dilemma. Do they tell the whole truth to all parties and split the commission 50/50 with a buyer's agent, or do they make sure they have the winning offer and keep the entire commission. Remember, at 6% the commission is $6000 per $100,000 of value.

The listing agent suggested the selling price of $400,000.

➢ The dual agent has an opportunity to get both sides of the commission if she lists and sells the same house.

➢ The dual agent, now working with both seller and buyer, tells the buyer they must at least come up to $375,000 in order to buy the home because of the competing offer. Soon the offers are presented and both seller and buyer agree to meet at $375,000. Everyone is happy and the house is sold.

Wait a minute!

Another potential buyer signed an offer at $370,000. That buyer probably would have come up in price too - maybe to full price or more. The seller is seriously damaged. The dual agent appears to be working to get their own offer accepted which also results in receiving the entire, undivided commission, instead of working in the seller's best interest.

➢ The dual agent got both sides of the commission.

➢ The buyer may have been pressured into paying more than they were comfortable with.

➢ The outside agent was not given the facts required to give his client an opportunity to pay more and get the home they wanted.

➢ The outside buyer was not treated with honesty.

> **Integrity can be seen, but not claimed.**

➢ The seller may have lost $25,000 or more.

➢ Your agent's honesty and integrity is critical as she will have a large amount of power over what may be the largest asset in your portfolio.

SELLING A HOUSE WITH AN AGENT

The majority of home sellers take on the task with a real estate agent. They feel that it is better to entrust the sale of their biggest investment to a professional, rather than learn about selling their biggest asset through trial and error.

Many people prefer to use an agent rather than deal with the complex legal and financial issues of today's real estate transaction.

Some advantages of working with agents include: access to the multiple listings allowing large numbers of buyers to have access to the house, expert advertising and management of the process including negotiation.

Deciding whether or not to use an agent has everything to do with you. If you feel fully confident that you can handle all the details, then sell your house on your own. If not, select a great agent that communicates well with you.

Who is your agent? Your neighbor or your ex-step cousin who is really nice….. No! So how do you choose an agent who will be effective? Ask the agents you interview questions to determine if they possess the ability and the philosophies that work for *you.*

IF YOU LIST, LIST WITH AN EXCELLENT AGENT

Choose a professional, successful, quality agent. The key to finding a quality agent is knowledge. Find one who is able to clearly explain:

➢ Their profession

➢ The current market

➢ Their marketing plan for your home

➢ How to stage

➢ Exactly how to prepare your house for a top dollar sale

➢ What to expect during the process

➢ What professional services they offer

➢ Every form, in detail, that you are asked to sign

➢ Great real estate agents prepare an accurate statistical pricing analysis specific to your home's condition, location and market only <u>after</u> they have seen the interior. The analysis does not have to be long or fancy. It has to be clear, understandable and useful.

RESEARCH PLAN

1.   Ask family, friends and co-workers about agents they
      have used to SELL a home.

2.   Check newspapers, home magazines and local agent
      web sites.

3.   Talk to escrow agents. They know who closes the
      most sales, using honesty, diligence and reason. They
      also know who the jerks are.

4.   Find agents with organized, logical, useful ads for their
      listings, not for the agent

5.   Go to open houses to look for agents that do their job,
      not agents who want to be your friend.

REMEMBER

Your agent (you?) must work patiently with **every person**.
You will be available at unreasonable hours and understand
that each person has their own style. Buyers and sellers
have "personality" conflicts but the agent (you?) selling your
home must ignore personality issues and stick to business.

➢ Even a jerk can afford your house. Ignore that attitude
   rather than reacting. You will move into your future
   and the jerk stays in your past!

➢ Unshaven, dirty t-shirt wearers can afford homes

➢ All races, all ages, all style of people ……. can afford
   homes. Your home is now a product for sale and it
   does not matter to you who buys it. From today
   forward, see and refer to your home as a house.

AGENT NEGOTIATION SKILLS TEST

How well does the agent represent their own position?

➢   Will he lower the listing commission?

➢   Will he take a short term listing?

➢   Will he accept an overpriced listing?

If they can not negotiate top dollar for themselves, a reasonable listing term and a reasonable price, the agent will probably not be able to negotiate well for you.

Do not damage yourself by selecting an agent based on the lowest commission and the highest suggested selling price.

SELLING A HOUSE CAN BE VERY PROFITABLE

Paying a commission _may_ make you the most money. Sell your house in the way that works best for your lifestyle. I am a licensed and highly experienced Washington State Real Estate Broker, yet I often contract with agents to sell my real estate. Why? I am so busy training people just like you exactly how to manage their own real estate that a great agent is more focused and does a better job than I can on my own property.

MEET and talk with property owners to understand their motivation and goals in <u>this specific</u> sale.

INSPECT the <u>entire</u> property, ask questions, photograph inside and out, feature individual property strengths and personality. Find the presentation focus inside and out. Take flattering photographs that show off the property and allow it to be recognized on "drive up."

ANALYZE the property for the highest and best use. What family style, age group, employment group is most likely to buy this house? The marketing created to attract a young family is very different in style and placement than marketing designed to attract retirees or a developer.

OBTAIN DATA that includes plat map, utility records, floor plan, septic as-built, well log, property profile, covenants, easement, shared well agreements, access agreements and every other detail. This information can be obtained at your city or county building and planning office, the assessor office, your insurance company, the Department of Ecology, the Health Department and other agencies. Yes, information gathering is a bit of a treasure hunt. All this information should go into the "Home Book" which will be kept open on the table or kitchen counter during every showing for the shopper's review.

Seven SUPER AGENT LISTING SERVICES

INVESTIGATE VALUE from active, pending, SOLD, withdrawn and expired listings of properties of similar age, style, condition and neighborhood.

PLAN and IMPLEMENT a flexible marketing system:

➢ Analyze who will be the logical buyer.

➢ Know how much the probable buyer can afford.

➢ Create a plan for the probable buyer to find this particular house.

➢ Describe what will make this house rise above the competition.

➢ Prepare a marketing plan, marketing materials and marketing schedule.

➢ Plan and maintain locations for the yard signs, directional signs and feature box.

➢ Advertise and hold creative open houses. Track and follow up on every contact.

➢ Hold a special open house for your neighbors and anyone else who happens to stop by when they see the open house sign.

CONTACT, CONTACT, CONTACT! Weekly conversations with each party to a listing or sales transaction are vital.

FSBO or Professional Agent Test

Grade yourself against the agents you interview. Be honest.
Add up the scores. Score: 0 = poor, 1 = fair, 2 = good, 3 = great.

WHICH AGENT WILL EARN YOU TOP DOLLAR?	1	2	3	YOU
Professional and comfortable with all people.				
Realistically have the time to get your house sold.				
Familiar with your neighborhood.				
Willing and able to price your home so it will sell.				
Has advertising & marketing ability.				
Knows how to listen.				
Determined and decisive.				
Wants to be your agent, not your friend or relative.				
How many homes did you sell last year?				
Are you a full time agent?				
How did you arrive at the suggested listing price?				
What is the marketing plan for this house?				
Written guarantee on frequency of contacts to you.				
Does **NOT** agree to lower their commission				
Has the integrity to represent your home.				
Has a positive, direct, ambitious manner..				
Are you a multiple listing service member?				
What is your philosophy on co-brokerage?				
Has the strength to tell you the whole truth.				
Understands you are the boss, they are the expert..				
Prepared to show you exactly how they do their job.				
TOTALS. The highest number is your agent.				

WHAT REAL ESTATE AGENTS REALLY WANT

The same thing everyone else wants with their work including appreciation, money and success. Real estate is a very competitive business. Some agents are experts. Some are incompetent. Some see the huge opportunity to manipulate your sale for their personal highest gain.

Every real estate transaction is made up of personalities and it is usually the personalities of one or more of the players that cause the most difficult problems. Some real estate transactions are very simple and some are not. There is often no way to tell which way it will go, but the more preparation and professionalism you establish at the beginning, the better your odds of a smooth transaction.

WHY LISTING AGREEMENTS LAST SO LONG

Real estate agents invest their cash in the marketing of your home on the bet the home will sell and they will earn a commission. If your home does not sell, the listing was a total loss of the time and marketing dollars the agent invested. The agent worked for nothing. Markets can be hot or cold. Houses can be priced just right or really wrong.

Sellers can be slow getting the house ready to sell or uncooperative about showings. The selling season may never arrive. A long listing period is a way of framing the agent's investment for a more likely profitable outcome.

RIGHTS YOU SIGN AWAY BY LISTING

You have signed away the right to sell your home without paying a commission. You, as the property owner, have the exclusive right to accept, counter offer or reject an offer. Your agent must present all offers to you.

IS IT OK TO FIRE A LISTING AGENT?

The technically correct answer to this question is NO.

The realistic answer is that most agents will absolutely put a listing on hold, agreeing not to market or show the home and simply allow the listing to expire if you decide not to sell.

If the agent refuses to put the listing on hold, simply notify the agent in writing you want an increase in price to an impossible level and remove permission for signs or other marketing.

If your agent has broken the listing agreement in substance and you want to move the listing to a different agent or agency, you must work with the broker or head of the real estate agency to obtain a written, signed and dated document rescinding the listing agreement.

REAL ESTATE COMMISSIONS

A Seller pays the listing commission when the Seller's property transfers to the new owner.

Commissions are typically contracted at a specific percentage of the selling price. Although commissions are certainly negotiable, residential rates seem to average at 6 percent. The value of the property, marketing and time investments, can have an effect on the rate. Even though commission rates may not be fixed among a group of real estate companies, the rate does tend to be extremely similar throughout a given market simply due to competitive pressure.

Each commission is split between brokerage and agent. Commonly a new agent may split each commission with their brokerage 50/50, while experienced agents split is 70/30 or 80/20. Some brokerages offer a 100% commission in exchange for a "desk fee and expenses."
When a house is actually sold by an agent other than the listing agent, the contracted commission is split (usually 50/50) with the buyer's agency. The listing agent may actually end up with 25% or less of the commission paid.

Be willing to offer strong commissions to strong agents. I do it and it is worth it. A great test to see how well your chosen agent will negotiate for you is to see how well they represent themselves.

Agreeing to lower the commission rate is a good sign of a bad negotiator.

COMMISSIONS CAN WORK AGAINST YOU

"$1000 Selling Agent Bonus!"   When a determined seller offers to pay the buyer's agent extra for procuring a buyer, that seller runs a high risk of a greedy listing agent discouraging other agents from writing offers so the listing agent does not have to split the commission or give away the bonus. I've seen that and more.....

BIG LIE #1: "It's sold." This, upon serious questioning means an offer has been written by the listing agent, but not yet accepted. This is a situation where the listing agent must bring all offers to the seller, but in fact is attempting, at a serious cost to the seller, to keep all the commission by discouraging other agents from writing an offer. Excellent agents understand that by working honestly with all agents they sell more listings faster and make the most money.

BIG LIE #2: "Oh, that property is no longer available." This can actually mean the listing term expired, when, in fact, the seller still wants to sell but the agent no longer has a listing agreement.

BIG LIE #3: "I'm sorry, a different offer was accepted." This is a tough one, because a buyer agent can not force a listing agent to disclose an accepted price until the sale actually closes. I have seen multiple offer situations where the seller accepted low offers because the higher offers written by buyer agents were never presented.

All buyer agents should insist upon presenting their offers directly to the seller. All sellers should insist upon a personal presentation of every offer by the buyer agent that wrote the offer.

BIG LIE # 4: "Sorry, the owner has received 3 offers and is not accepting any others." At least in Washington, all offers must be presented to the seller.

BIG LIE #5: "The selling side of the commission is 2%." In reality the full commission is 7%. This listing agent makes sure to keep the large share of the commission. The actual result of this behavior is that buyer agents learn quickly not to show that agent's listings.

BIG LIE #6: "The seller will not allow you to present your own offer. Sellers benefit from presentation of each offer by the buyer agent with the opportunity to ask questions and gain inside information regarding each buyer to make informed counter-offer decisions.

BIG LIE #7: "The owner is out of town. I will present the offer as soon as I can." This is a delay tactic used so the listing agent can get the entire commission by procuring a buyer of their own in spite of the extreme risk of losing buyer number one.

This is done to get an offer the listing agent wrote accepted before they have to present the second offer. The buyer agent who wrote the offer also faces a dilemma. If the buyer agent gives the offer to the listing agent immediately, the listing agent has all the facts they need to procure a higher offer. If the buyer agent holds the offer until they can present it them self, the listing agent can work hard to write an offer and have it accepted before they tell the buyer agent that the seller is available.

The Great Agent Creed

- ☑ Serve each client with honesty, diligence and common sense.

- ☑ Use all the skills I possess to research the best solution for each client.

- ☑ Take notes on every contact, call and situation.

- ☑ Give my clients full disclosure.

- ☑ Work in my client's best interest at all times.

- ☑ Work within the law.

- ☑ Call back on every message.

- ☑ Keep every file organized.

- ☑ Meet each commitment.

- ☑ Help my client understand both sides of every issue.

- ☑ Use my professionalism, reason, and expertise to prepare clients and their homes for a top dollar sale.

- ☑ Work honestly with every buyer and agent.

- ☑ Strive for education and updated information.

Maintain an agent book that offers a true reflection of my personal commitment to the client. This book may include work philosophy; resume; forms; samples; management and marketing plans; and client testimonials.

☑   Obtain all available data including plat map, septic, covenants, well, property profile, easement, shared well agreements and access agreements on every listing.

☑   Investigate value based on SOLD comparable homes while using active, pending SOLD, withdrawn and expired homes to assess the competition.

☑   Listen carefully to hear the motivation and goals of each client in their specific sale.

☑   Inspect the <u>entire</u> property.

☑   Take excellent photos that show the home's personality.

☑   Analyze property for its highest and best use.

☑   Regularly submit updated data to the seller on marketing the market, contacts and price.

☑   Manage paperwork, systems, signs and marketing.

☑   Create open houses that draw buyers.

☑   Negotiate all offers according to the client's instructions.

TOOLS NEEDED TO LIST YOUR OWN HOME

CAMERA (DIGITAL IS BEST): Photograph your completely staged home inside and out. Carefully frame each shot. There can be no garbage cans, power poles, wires, toys in the yard, cat on the bed, open cabinets or dishes in the sink. Potential buyers who see your photos should be eager to walk through that beautiful *home.*

TAPE MEASURE / TABLET / PEN: Follow the forms in this book to inspect every inch of the house and property. I strongly recommend you look first at your old appraisal. Is there a floor plan sketch you can copy to use for advertising? If not, you will need to draw one. Graph paper and a ruler make drawing a basic floor plan easy. Buy ¼ inch grid graph paper. Each little square represents 1 foot. Begin with the outside of the house and then fill in the rooms. Place a notation on your drawing that it is approximate and not guaranteed for accuracy. Use a ruler to draw straight lines. Rough sketch while you measure the house, then redraw the sketch with all the quality you can muster.

Place disclaimers on every informational page you create, because you are human and will make a mistake somewhere.

FLASHLIGHT: Look carefully at every nook, crawl space and attic space in your house. Look for problems and fix them. Look for opportunities and highlight them. Your job here is much more important than the display person at a top end department store. Your goal is to help buyers see the joy and comfort that will become part of their daily life when they are the proud owners of the house you sell them.

STAGING: The quality of your home staging determines whether you will get a *Top Dollar Sale*, an average price or a distressed sale price. When preparing to sell you may need to hold a big yard sale for all the junk you really do not need. Pack up your collections, valuables and personal items. Clean, paint and finally create beauty and space. Be prepared to fall back in love with your house.

YARD SIGNS: Yes, Yes, Yes! Minimum size is 18 x 24. Place, simple, clean signs so they face oncoming traffic in a location that clearly shows which house is FOR SALE. Be proud of your work and your house. Embarrassed sellers make buyers wonder what is being hidden.

DIRECTIONAL SIGNS: Directional signs lead people who are intentionally looking for your house and lead other people who simply follow signs in hope of a great discovery.

COLLECT ALL THE PAPERWORK

➢ Obtain the county assessor and treasurer reports detailing the history and facts of your property. You want everything available including maps, values, taxes, square footage and all other information. These documents are available in public records for you and every savvy buyer.

➢ Ask the assessor's office for a list of comparable sales over the last 6 months. All counties will not do this for you, but most will. In many areas all the information you need is available on the assessor's website.

➢ Honestly review your neighborhood from the perspective of a buyer.

➢ Set your price.

➢ Create a complete feature sheet with disclaimers.

➢ Install signs immediately with a feature sheet box.

➢ Consider placing a lock box on your back door to enable buyer agents to show your home without your interference.

➢ Prepare your Home Book. The Home Book will be left open on the table for the buyer's inspection during every showing. See www.JuliDoty.com .

➢ They are not comfortable with the paperwork.

> FSBOs have trouble understanding and dealing with the contingencies and inspections requested by the buyer.

> FSBOs lack the experience and courage to know how and when to say, "Are you ready to write this up?"

> Defensive attitudes interfere with profitable interactions between buyer and seller.

To sell your house for top dollar you must shut up, get out of the way and allow home shoppers to look and feel the house on their own. Selling comes next, not during the showing.

YOU CAN BEAT THESE ODDS

National statistics report FSBO's commonly sell for 13% under market value! In my area that comes up to approximately a $32,000 loss.

FSBO homes take an average of 17 weeks to sell, which is one month longer than the national average for listed homes.

More than 50% of all FSBO's do not sell at all! Either they end up listing with a real estate agency or simply take their home off the market.

WHY FSBO'S WANT TO SELL WITHOUT AN AGENT

I have asked many FSBO's:

➢ Are you selling FSBO to save money?

➢ Do you hate real estate agents?

➢ What do you think a real estate agent really does?

And they actually answered:

➢ "I just want to try it myself, just for a while and then if it doesn't work, I'll list."

➢ "It's a lot of money, you know."

➢ "I hate real estate agents."

➢ "Agents get paid a huge commission for simply finding a buyer! They really don't do anything."

This entire book is devoted to telling you *exactly how to* sell by owner for top dollar. You will learn the secrets of *exactly how to* be a great FSBO! You get the tools that will allow you to do a great job. Whether you or an agent sells your house, the principals are the same

➢ Use advertising techniques that get results.

➢ Prepare your home to sell quickly.

➢ Create the World's Greatest Open House.

- ➢ Follow the Rule of Full Price.

- ➢ Create *urgency!*

- ➢ Use time to your advantage.

- ➢ Negotiate smart.

- ➢ Have lawyers, bankers, escrow officers and other professionals help you.

WHO SHOULD SELL YOUR HOUSE?

You, if you have the time and the determination to do a great job.

It is a huge amount of work where you absolutely must pay attention to every detail. If you can not or will not do a great job, then pay the commission. It is equal to what you might agree to as a small price reduction.

SAVE THE COMMISSION

By not paying a real estate commission, you have the potential to save big money. Your potential cash savings might be $30,000 or more. Some people wonder why less than 20% of home sellers undertake the task of selling their house on their own. The answer is clear. Selling by owner is a pot load of work and risk. The more you know, the better the job you will do.

Many home owners who consider a self sale of their house change their mind and hire a real estate agent when they see the level of

Sale Price	6% Commission
$ 100,000	$ 6,000
$ 200,000	12,000
$ 300,000	18,000
$ 400,000	24,000
$ 500,000	$ 30,000

knowledge and commitment needed to do an effective job.

Using the details given to you in The Secrets of Exactly How To FSBO and at www.JuliDoty.com you will successfully sell your house and save that commission.

ADVANTAGES OF FSBO SELLING

➤ There is no commission to pay.

➤ You are in total control of the transaction. If mistakes are made, they are your own. There is no one else to make mistakes "for" you.

➤ If you owe as much or more than your home is worth, paying a commission could force you to come up with cash at closing to cover all the expenses of the sale.

➤ You are at the house and available for showings.

DISADVANTAGES OF FSBO SELLING

➤ You must rely on your own instincts.

➤ Marketing and advertising costs are your own, which can be expensive.

➤ Without access to the multiple listing service you must hunt for buyers one at a time.

➤ Without all the tools in hand, you may under-price or over-price the house.

➤ If you are an unskilled negotiator, you may leave money on the table.

➤ Responsibility for paperwork and legal forms is yours.

➤ A serious amount of time must be devoted to doing a great FSBO job.

➤ Some buyers will ask for a discount "since you are not paying a commission."

SELL YOUR HOME FOR TOP DOLLAR

1.   <u>Don't scrimp</u> on your house preparation. You will be in competition with houses listed by agents who coach their clients on all aspects of preparing their home for a top dollar sale.

2.   Be aware of the legal requirements for disclosure in your state. Not disclosing necessary information or not using the correct form could leave you at risk for legal action from a buyer.

3.   Become an expert in advertising and marketing. Make your house stand out!

4.   Familiarize yourself with **offers** and **contracts** now-- don't wait until you have one in your hand.

5.   Be aware of equal housing laws. Not only is discrimination stupid (you limit your potential market), it's illegal!

6.   Prepare yourself to sell your home. Do your best to see the house, no longer as your home, but as a product to be marketed. Only refer to it as a house. This takes work, especially if you have built years of memories. Know that you will keep your memories, but a separation in your mind is necessary, if you want to maximize to a Top Dollar Sale.

7.   Decide whether it is to your advantage to sell your house <u>with an agent</u> or <u>by owner</u>.

8.   *Get a whole house inspection*. This inspection is designed to uncover major defects before they can cause trouble with a potential buyer and to describe maintenance that will be needed. It is also a signal to buyers that you are a responsible seller.

9.   *Prepare the house*. Stand back and look at your house as objectively as possible. Would you buy this home? Ask friends and neighbors to do the same, asking them to be totally honest. Overlooking flaws can cost you money! Get them fixed before you put the house on the market.

10.   Do what is necessary to make your house *stand out from the competition*. Make certain that your house is fresher, cleaner and better maintained. Familiarize yourself with effective marketing and advertising techniques.

11.   Price your house very close to market value. Pulling a price "out of the air" is almost never successful. The fastest top dollar sales happen when the house is priced right – right from the start.

12. *Remove the "imprint"* you have made on the house. Buyers must be able to envision themselves in the house, which is nearly impossible if everywhere they turn they see you!

13. Know what you can and cannot change about your house. This allows you to concentrate on those items that will bring the highest reward.

14. Time you spend staging and preparing your home for sale is valuable. Do it!

15. File all the receipts for your home improvements. These can be valuable in tax saving.

16. Prepare a Home Book that includes the inspection reports, county records, utility report, seasonal pictures, disclosure statements and other valuable information on your home. This will be left open for perusal by any interested party.

17. Have a big yard sale *before* you show your home. Junk makes your house appear and feel small. Sell, donate or throw away everything you don't need. (There is a reason I underlined the word need.)

18. Become familiar with Home Warranty Programs. Some buyer agents highly recommend them to their client. My advice, should you be requested to provide this policy is to calculate the cost into closing and say yes! If something were to happen, such as a major mechanical failure of the heat system right after closing, the ability of the buyer to place a claim on you would certainly be affected.

19.   Be very knowledgeable about financing options.

20.   Follow the rules for showing your home.

21.   Understand the entire transaction from the buyer's point of view. Only then will you be an effective negotiator.

22.   Be as flexible as possible in your moving plans. Some buyers will need 90 days to get their financing ready for closing, some will have cash and want to close and move in within two weeks.

23.   Keep reading. Your answers are here and at www.**JuliDoty.com**.

DECISION TIME

SELL BY-AGENT OR BY-OWNER?

You must make your decision to sell by owner based on an honest assessment of your personality and abilities. Not everyone is good at selling their own home.

A Prepared FSBO is Willing and Able To:

1.   Put signs in your front yard and at street corners leading to your home.

2.   Allow potential buyers to look <u>without interference</u>.

3.   Allow potential buyers privacy and emotional space when they are looking at your house. In the first showing, buyers usually do not care where the water comes in to the house or what brand of furnace you have. Stay back, let them look, give them a tablet and have them come ask anything that want to know when they are done looking. The buyer is looking for a home that fills their heart or their needs. The details come later.

4.   Follow up – CALL – every person that looks at your house with a thank you call. Ask them if they have any questions or would like a second look. Ask if they have any suggestions for you. Be nice. Even if they don't like your house, they may know the person who will.

5. Do the research and present it to every buyer only at the moment they are ready for it. Not before. The best way to do this is to make and use a Home Book.

6. Manage open negotiation while fully understanding the other side.

7. Track deadlines.

8. Solve problems.

9. Work with difficult personalities with patience and joy.

10. Coordinate inspectors, appraisers, the title company and other professionals at their convenience.

11. Understand the nuances of all the documents from research to purchase and sale agreements to closing documents.

12. Prepare all advertising which includes writing quality ads, proper sign placement, promotion of the house and preparation for all events.

13. See their house realistically (this is tougher than you think!).

14. Read and understand the behavior of each potential buyer, treating each one individually.

15. Not take anything that happens personally.

BEAT THE ODDS

Costs come in many ways. Cash, certainly, but the emotion, stress, fear and insecurity that arrive with placing your home on the market can be overwhelming. As time drags on with no offers, your neighbors, friends and family all begin saying, "Is your house **still not sold**"?

Statistics tell us more than half of FSBO properties end up listed with a real estate agent. On average, even those homes who sell FSBO sell for 13% less than homes listed by real estate agents. Compared to a six percent commission you may be left with a lower net at closing.

Your job is to beat the odds. You must sell at the highest price with the lowest costs.

MOVING 101

PLAN YOUR MOVE

Moving is easiest when you can do it all at once, but that is not how it always works.

When selling by owner you have a pre-moving opportunity to increase the value of your house. As an important part of preparing your home for sale have a big yard sale to get rid of the extra stuff. Donate or dispose of the things you do not sell.

Pack your collections and valuables into boxes that are marked and ready for moving. Designate one corner of the garage or storage building to hold these boxes.

This is about to become the easiest move ever.

TOOLS AND SUPPLIES

- ➢ Rent an appliance dolly to load appliances and other heavy objects.
- ➢ Collect boxes for your move that are a similar shape and size. Try to box everything. The better you package your belongings the better they will travel. All boxes used for packing need to have tops. Free boxes are great. You can get them from liquor stores, supermarkets or your office. Copy paper boxes are a wonderful size and offer the benefit of handles. You can buy boxes from a truck rental or moving company.

- ➢ Mark each box with the room it will be moved into.

- ➢ Include moving terms in the purchase and sale agreement that give the Seller 3 days occupancy after closing in the SOLD house.

- ➢ Continue to pack up and clean as you move through the selling process. You will be surprised how much of your stuff is just, "stuff".

- ➢ Large rolls of 2-inch packing tape and a tape gun.

- ➢ Rope, cord or tie straps

- ➢ Box or utility knife

- ➢ Marking pens to label your boxes.

- ➢ Plastic bags or shrink wrap to protect your belongings.

- ➢ Newspaper, cardboard, and towels for padding.

OTHER MOVING IDEAS

➢ Disassemble all items you can.

➢ **Move out early, if possible.**

➢ Do not ship flammable items, liquids or other materials that will spill, spoil or leak. Empty the propane tank from barbecue grill and properly drain garden hoses.

➢ Label each box with the room it came from and its contents.

➢ Load heavy appliances securely against the front wall of the trailer and secure them.

➢ Use loose cushions, pillows and blankets as pads between furniture to prevent rubbing.

➢ Mark appropriate boxes with a large easy to read "FRAGILE".

➢ Pad all furniture with blankets or bubble wrap. Secure padding to furniture. When possible, remove the legs from furniture and place all bolts/screws in a plastic bag and tape it to the bottom of the furniture. If you need blankets most charitable organizations sell regular quilts and blankets for a very reasonable price. You can rent moving pad from some truck rental places. Flattened cardboard boxes make great dividers between artwork, mirrors and furniture.

➢ Secure drawers of furniture from opening.

➢　Try to keep boxes to 50 pounds or less and always lift with your legs. Tape the bottom of all boxes to make certain they will hold your belongings. It is also recommended that the top of the boxes be taped shut to ensure that it will not open while being loaded, unloaded or while in transit.

➢　Whenever possible, use the original shipping boxes for televisions, computers, stereo equipment and other electronics. Boxed items travel much better.

➢　Cover paintings carefully to protect them in transit.

➢　It is dangerous and illegal to transport flammable and hazardous materials. If you have any flammable or combustible materials dispose of them properly. This includes propane, kerosene, gasoline, motor oil, paint, turpentine, etc.

LOAD THE MOVING TRUCK

➢　Load heavy items on bottom, lighter items on top.

➢　Load items tightly to prevent shifting, rubbing or puncturing during transit. Use blankets and other protective wrapping to protect your

➢　Use your space well.

➢　Tie everything off! Movement causes damage.

FORECLOSURE

Act now. Call your lender and find out all the facts and discuss all the options. This is the time to be courteous, listen well for hints that might offer opportunities, and keep in mind at all times that the person on the phone with you is only doing their job.

> What will it cost today to reinstate the loan?

> Does your lender have any special programs that can allow you to get back on track over a period of time?

> If you face any serious issue that affects your home you may be under a bucket load of stress.
>
> Help is here.

> Will your lender place your old debt at the back of the loan so you become current today? This is especially useful when you have been out of work for a time, but can now resume making regular payments.

> Some lenders will entirely forgive the past due debt.

> Some lenders will allow you to pay your regular payment plus an additional amount with each payment to allow you time to catch up.

➢ Make sure you understand all the dates and deadlines.

➢ Make sure you have a copy of <u>all</u> paperwork including the lender commitment. Get everything in writing!

➢ Make sure your credit report will show your payments as current as long as you stick to your agreements.

Let's take a moment to be very real. What can you actually do? Can you make all future payments on time? Can you afford to move? If you do not make any more payments how long until you are evicted? Will that give you enough money to move? Your final day of occupancy will typically be 20 days after the house is sold on the courthouse steps (or other location). If you are in this situation, go to **JuliDoty.com** for my free report on Foreclosure Options, Warnings and Opportunities.

Now, let's make some decisions. Were you able to make agreements with the lender that will allow you to keep the home?

Yes? Great. Make sure you keep the agreement you made.

No? OK. The next thing the lender may agree to is to allow you to forestall the actual foreclosure for a few months while you work hard to sell the house. They may insist you list with an agent. Call now and set this up with your lender.

Believe me it is easier to do it now than to ignore it.

BANKRUPTCY

Bankruptcy is not a cure for financial problems. It is more like pushing a "pause" button that allows you a bit of time to get reorganized and resolve the problem that got you to bankruptcy. A huge percentage of the people who file are simply looking for the temporary relief, not the permanent fix. I want you to be special.

Investigate the different types of bankruptcy. Know the differences.

When you file for bankruptcy a "stay" is placed on any foreclosure proceedings against you. That stay will soon be lifted and the foreclosure will proceed unless you are able to bring your home loan current and keep it current.

Even when a foreclosure is resolved during bankruptcy, it is often reinstated in the next few months because the debtor simply did not change the behavior that got them into bankruptcy in the first place.

What behavior got you into bankruptcy? Unemployment? Overspending, over generosity, a fear of disappointing others, competitiveness, anger or mismanaged emotional pain?

What happened? Why do you feel that way? Is it really important once you think about it clearly? No? Ok, stop it. Simply stop the stupid behavior that gets you into financial trouble. I say "stupid" because I've had my own share of stupid behaviors. Usually those behaviors are symptoms of serious issues such as:

- Divorce

- Death of a loved one

- Illness

These three are tough. Divorce we will talk about in a minute but let's deal with the last two. I lost my daughter, my step son, my step father, both grandmas and grandpas and a very dear cousin. Honor those you love by living and loving. My family, alive and passed, would not want me to "abuse myself in their honor."

Neither would yours. Move forward steadily with your future and remember, with joy, the great moments and lessons of your past.

Illness is something we must deal with. Is the illness temporary or is it permanent? You have the option to simply choose to enjoy the life and health you do have.

If temporary, bankruptcy may be the cure you need to get back on track. If your illness is permanent, will it affect your income? If so, you must make some immediate changes.

Do not allow any situation to control you. Gain complete understanding of the situation so you can make smart and practical decisions. Never allow over-emotional people to stop you from doing what is right.

DIVORCE

Thousands of books are written to analyze and help people through the pain of divorce. Divorce is a common cause for high stress emergent home sales. A single income will no longer make the house payment and there is no longer time to do the maintenance.

If you are considering divorce, first consider my **highly condensed** philosophy on divorce. "Divorce is commonly caused by one person's unwillingness to change the very habit they will change soon after the divorce."

➢ Weight

➢ Cheating

➢ Overspending

➢ Nagging or .....

Talk about it, fix it, stay married and be happy. If that fails, get divorced and be happy.

In a divorce caused house sale, open communication is profitable for everyone. Put every agreement between (ex)spouses in writing. Meet with professionals working on the sale of the house. Ask them to report to both parties. Do not attempt to manipulate values or stall a sale. Get the house sold equitably and move forward with your individual lives.

OTHER STRESS FACTORS

HOUSE TOO SMALL

Often a house is too small simply because it holds too much junk. Begin with a huge yard sale and staging event. Once staged, you may like your house much better.

Now decide if you want to stay in that home, move up or remodel. You are ready for any choice.   Do a financial analysis of each idea and go with the best plan for you.

HOUSE TOO BIG

➢   Sell.

➢   Rent out one level or one part of the house.

➢   Open a home-based business and make some money with that excess square footage.

➢   Carefully consider asking a family member or friend to share the house and expenses.

REMODEL OR MOVE?

The answer to this question is in the details. Think about both sides and write down the pros and cons.

Remodeling means mess and extra work - so does moving. Consider how much more your home may be worth if you do some improvements and then sell it. Your decision will become obvious.

> **Remodel:** The house and location are great. It just needs a master bedroom and better kitchen.

> **Move:** It's a long drive to work. I could make lots of money, if I sold right now. There is a house near my work that I can get cheap and remodel!

WHEN A NEIGHBOR IS *IMPOSSIBLE!*

> Report illegal activity to police.

> Assess who the real jerk is. It just might be you. Attempt to resolve your differences. Understand that neighbor disputes are one of the top causes of court cases. Law suits are almost always a really bad idea.

> Build a tall fence and ignore them.

> Move. Happiness and safety are very important.

WHEN YOU ARE SELLING A FAMILY ESTATE

Families feud over real estate. Siblings fight, disagree on price and style and eventually the ONE that does all the work is mad at the OTHERS for not helping and the OTHERS are mad at the ONE for doing all the work wrong. Family is too important to get into this trauma.

LONG DISTANCE SELLING

A quality local agent will perform much better than a friend or neighbor.   Get agent referrals for a professional agent if you can not do the job yourself.

Seven KEYS TO A SUCCESSFUL SALE

1.   *The Rule of Full Price*

Price your home very close to market value. Many
home owners are afraid they will leave money on the
table if they do not ask an exorbitant price.   Price your
house at market value and leave a bit of room for a
small negotiation so the buyer can feel like a winner.
Use this method to become a successful and savvy
real estate seller.

2.   *Stage Every House You Sell*

Beauty, comfort and cleanliness add significant dollars
to the sale price.

3.   *Leave When an Agent Shows Your House*

Greet the agent and their client, hand them each a
feature sheet and leave.

4.   *Hold a Neighborhood Open House*

Proudly invite your friends and neighbors to your home
for a special two hour open house. Serve fresh,
homemade lemonade. Your goal with this open house
is to have every one of those friends think about who
should live there. I have sold many homes exactly this
way.

5   *Know the Rules before You Need Them*

Real estate laws are very specific. Obtain preprinted forms from www.JuliDoty.com that are approved for your state prior to showing your property. Read those forms carefully. Understand the negotiation points. Know what you are signing. Contracts are legally binding and mistakes can cost you big money. Research your state laws for disclosure regulations or check www.JuliDoty.com.

6.   *Be Proud Selling Your House*

Yard signs are critical selling tools. Make yours stand as straight and tall as you do when you proudly show your home to friends, neighbors, agents and buyers.

7.   *Appraised Value and Market Value May Not be the Equal*

Appraisals are usually prepared to support a proposed purchase or refinance amount. The appraiser has the flexibility to select sales which support the requested value, while ignoring distressed and motivated sales.

When shopping for a home, a buyer will not ignore lower priced homes and they may see your house as very over priced.

REAL ESTATE, REAL ADVICE
Exactly How To

Finance

2

**Buyer Financing
Your Existing Loan**

BUYER FINANCING

HOW MUCH HOUSE
CAN YOUR BUYER AFFORD?

You may think this is not your problem, but it is.

Most purchase and sale agreements include a "Financing Addendum." This document describes the terms under which a buyer has a legal responsibility to buy your house. If the buyer's financing fails, the buyer gets the earnest money returned and the buyer walks away, unscathed.

If you, the seller have spent 30 – 60 days or more packing, planning your own move but not finding a backup buyer, you get to start all over again, maybe in a market that is not as great as it was. Your house is not sold until it is closed.

Request a written copy of the pre-approval letter from the buyers that make an offer. Talk to them with a smile, and in a conversational manner, about their job and their plans. Get to know them. You will learn useful information, if you really listen.

GENERAL LOAN GUIDELINES

A monthly real estate mortgage payment that includes principal, interest, property taxes and insurance should not be more than 28 percent of the gross monthly income.

Total debt should not be more than 36 percent of your gross income and includes mortgage payment, car loans, child support and alimony, credit card bills, student loans, etc.

Some loans (typically with a higher interest rate, may have more lenient debt to income ratios.

PROPERTY TAX AND HOMEOWNER INSURANCE

Taxes are part of a monthly house payment, whether paid privately or through the mortgage payment. Buyers must insure your property to

Gross Income	28% of Monthly Income	36% of Monthly Income
$20,000	$467	$600
$30,000	$700	$900
$40,000	$933	$1200
$50,000	$1,167	$1,500
$60,000	$1,400	$1,800
$80,000	$1,867	$2,400
$100,000	$2,333	$3,000
$150,000	$3,500	$4,500

obtain a mortgage. As you calculate a potential buyer's actual ability to buy your house consider the cost of real estate taxes and insurance.

INTEREST RATES MATTER

The following chart shows the maximum loan amount which borrowers qualify for based on their annual gross salary, the amount of down payment they have saved and their other debt. Home loan interest is calculated on the amount of principal remaining on the loan. Take a close look at a $100,000 home loan.

Your home might be worth $300,000 or you may want to buy a home that is $400,000. The numbers just get proportionally larger. At $100,000 the math is easy to follow.

During the first 20 years of real estate investing I paid interest at the rate of 11-12%. Even at those rates that seem exorbitant today, those properties were very profitable.

30 Year Fixed Rate Loan of $100,000	5.5% Interest	11% Interest	15% Interest
Monthly Payment	$568	$942	$1265
Term	30 Years	30 Years	30 Years
Amount Paid Over Term of Loan	$204,000	$343,000	$455,000

IS THE BUYER PRE-QUALIFIED?

In order to estimate the amount of mortgage a borrower can qualify for, a lender will evaluate a homebuyer's credit history, how much they earn, how much they have saved, how much they owe and the amount of time they have held the same line of work.

Prequalification is based on what the borrower tells the lender and it offers no guarantees of the buyer's ability to purchase your home.

…. OR PRE-APPROVED?

In a pre-approved home loan the lender verifies the information supplied by the borrower. In return, the borrower receives a letter stating they have mortgage approval for a certain amount. This approval is subject to the borrower having no change in their employment or financial status. The actual purchase of your home is subject to your house passing an appraisal and any required inspections.

CARS, TRUCKS AND TOYS

A recent purchase of a vehicle can seriously affect the ability to buy a house. It can lower the buyer's credit rating and increase the debt-to-income ratio. The quality and timing of your buyer's financing is critical to your successful real estate transaction.

BUYER FINANCING MATTERS

If that financing fails, so does your sale. Your future is placed on hold – maybe unnecessarily. The earnest money placed on the sale may be contingent on financing and so well protected that the buyer has no pressure to complete the sale.

LOCK-INS

"Locking in" a rate or points at the time of application or during the processing of a loan will keep the rate and/or points from changing until the loan closes with the purchase of a house or property.

MORTGAGE INSURANCE

Private mortgage insurance and government mortgage insurance protect the lender against default and enable the lender to make a loan which is considered higher risk.

YOUR EXISTING LOAN

SHOULD YOU MAKE A PAYMENT NEAR CLOSING?

Always keep your payments current. Your escrow officer will get an exact payoff amount at closing. Any payment that is "in the mail" will be refunded.

WHO PAYS OFF YOUR CURRENT LOAN?

The closing company will work directly with your lender. Your current home loan will be paid off at the time the sale closes. You will give permission, in writing, to your closing officer to handle this process for you.

CONSIDER CARRYING THE CONTRACT

➢ When you prefer to earn interest and receive monthly payments

➢ In a buyers market

➢ When you have substantial real estate holdings

➢ When you are confident of the buyer's ability to continue to make their payments

➢ When the buyer has a substantial down payment

Instead of paying interest, you are now in the power position of the bank, earning interest. I advise all my clients who offer financing to their buyers to use an escrow service to collect, disperse and track payments.

When there is more than one loan on a house, the loans have priority (1st position, 2nd position, etc.) for repayment based on their time of recording at the auditor's office. Does it matter whether you are in 1ST or 2nd position? YES!

Second position is only for those folks who are willing to bet their cash and real estate. Ideally, as seller, you will only go into second position in the case where you absolutely must sell or you can afford to lose the amount of money on your second position loan.

MAY A SELLER REQUEST A CREDIT REPORT?

Although it is not common, the Seller has the right to request, and the Buyer has the right to agree, or not agree, to the Seller's written request for a credit report.

A credit report is typically supplied to the Seller as one of the terms in the Purchase and Sale Agreement when the Seller offers to carry the contract, instead of the buyer applying for a bank loan.

Real Estate, Real Advice
Exactly How To

Work

Well

With

Buyers

3

Buyers
Buyer Agents

BUYERS

What exactly does a seller need? *A buyer!*

BUYER FEARS

You may wonder why you should care what buyers fear. For you to successfully sell your home, you must become a bit of a counselor.

Many fears stop buyers from ever writing an offer or following through on the offers they do write. Sometimes called "Buyer Remorse", this is something you must understand.

"Will I make the right decision?" This can result in unwillingness to make any decision.

"Should I buy an existing home or build a new one?" The answer lies in the strength of the buyer's personal life, their ability to wait about a year to go through the entire construction process and the price of land, materials and labor versus an existing home.

> If you want to find the most and keep the best buyers, you must understand and cater to buyers.
>
> When a seller completely understands the buyer side of the negotiation, the seller comes out a winner!

"Can I afford this house?"

"Is this house too good for me?" *Don't laugh*, this is a common secret fear!

Renters wonder, "Can I take care of my own home?"

"What are the hidden problems in this house"? This is the reason you prepare a Home Book that is left out and open during every showing!

"What if I hate the house after I move in?"

"What if I buy this house and then find something better"? This is a crippling emotional merry-go-round that buyers get over quickly or they don't.

PRE-QUALIFIED BUYERS

There are unwritten "rules" about showing homes only to "pre-qualified" buyers.

These rules can work for you – and against you. You never know in advance which showing will be the sale. People with money do not always show their net worth in the way they dress.

BUYERS COME IN MANY STYLES

> Some are looking for a great deal.

> Some need to move **now**.

> Some want to move – *eventually* - when they find the perfect home.

> Some buyers bring an agent who is contracted to work in the buyer's best interest.

> Every buyer will have their own style and taste. Do not expect everyone to love your home. Most will not love it. Don't take it personally. Keep a smile on your face like the perfect salesperson you are and keep showing that house.

THERE IS A BUYER FOR YOUR HOUSE.

You will encounter buyers who are determined, arrogant, unmotivated and unimpressive. I have met a number of buyers and sellers who, when describing their real estate abilities said in defeat, "Oh, I always buy high and sell low! My luck is awful!" What is awful is not their luck, it is their investigational and decision making practices.

But, the buyer you really need to understand is the Buy Low, Sell High Buyer.

THE BUY LOW, SELL HIGH BUYER (BLSH)

Each buyer sets a price range and their agent shows them all the available homes. Then that buyer picks one, right? Wrong! The *Buy Low, Sell High Buyer* performs a market analysis on the value of every property they consider.

Key factors suggest to a *Buy Low, Sell High Buyer* that a "deal" may be had.

➢ Junk

➢ Bad smells

➢ Deferred maintenance

➢ A partially furnished house suggesting divorce

➢ An irritating seller that drives off most buyers

➢ Tenants or owners that talk way too much

➢ Disgruntled neighbors

➢ Utility or mortgage late notices left on the table during showings

➢ Signs of alcohol or drug use

➢ Signs of illness

A BLSH buyer understands immediately that the above signs mean a possible instant equity purchase may be available which can provide them with the opportunity for a line of credit or simply profit at sale.   Equity is the difference between what a property is worth and the amount of debt that is against it.

Instant equity simply means that the seller did not take advantage of the full value potential of his property before he sold it.

BUYERS ARE LOOKING FOR OPPORTUNITY

Many real estate investors buy one home after another, moving up by using equity in each house which the seller did not to take advantage of.

It is sad to understand that many distressed homes are owned by people in serious financial trouble that might be resolved by putting some effort into a clean up and profitable sale of their house. Instead, they allow the house to be sold very cheaply or even lost in foreclosure.

People in financial stress are often terrified of the truth and simply hide their way into foreclosure. Just imagine the buyer feeding frenzy that could solve every problem if a home owner were willing to write an ad something like the following:

> "I lost my job, my wife is ill and we must quickly sell our 3 bedroom, 2 bath, 1800 square foot home.
>
> We will sell this home to the buyer who brings us the most walk away cash, the fastest." Buyer must also pay off our current home loan of $76,000 plus all fees and closing costs.
>
> 303 Market Street, Julitown, WA   490.888.9999

The truth is a powerful tool that many people are <u>unwilling</u> to use.

In any negotiation give the buyer a way to win some details. Consider the power the next ad offers the Seller by subtly suggesting that some things are negotiable, but not price.

This could be used when you owe nearly what the house is worth, but you really must sell. Let the buyer win something else.

Classic lake shore home priced at $283,500.

Enjoy 2500 square foot stately home on North Shore surrounded by 3 acres of land. Appliances, furnishings and closing date are negotiable.

1214 Lake Shore Lane, Shannon, OH

To view, please call 509.777.3333

Some buyers may be looking for a deal. They may be looking for something other than what you offer. That is Ok. Thank them for coming by and tell them you hope they tell their friends about the opportunity to buy this house.

My Formatting Advice:

Always write ads with a left hand margin rather than centered. Centered writings may look nice, but reading them is too much work. Make it easy for your buyer to buy your house!

BUYER FINANCING ISSUES

If the buyer's financing fails, so does your sale. Your future could be unnecessarily placed on hold. Stay in contact with the lender so you know if any problems arise.

When a sale is contingent upon financing, the buyer will have a contracted number of days, commonly 30, during which they can back out of the sale and have the earnest money returned. Make sure the contract includes a clause stating the lender may provide the seller with information on the progress of the loan via telephone or email and that the lender must notify the seller personally, in writing, if, when and why the financing fails.

INSPECTIONS

Inspections and repairs should be scheduled as soon as you make the decision to sell your house. Do not wait for buyer discovery.

What about those problems you "just lived with"? Well, how did you price your house? Generally my advice is fix it, if you can afford it, otherwise disclose the material defects and sell AS-IS.

OPERATION

Make this sale the most pleasant experience ever, for all the people involved. The more reasonable you are the harder all the participants will work when it comes time to solve a problem.

SAY YES TO BUYER AGENTS

A buyer agent may approach you asking to show your home to one of their clients. Say yes. The buyer agent obviously wants to be paid for selling real estate for you, so you must deal with this issue in a successful straight forward manner.

A typical "untrained" FSBO response might be, "My price is $250,000. You can sell it, but your commission is on top. I want $250,000!"

Buyers are a rare and valuable commodity. Since most real estate agents are simply not experienced enough to deal with the problem you just created, you are about to lose a buyer.

Most real estate agents have never worked as a *professional* buyer agent. They do not have a contract with the buyer and are unwilling to ask the buyer to pay the commission on top of the selling price. What the buyer agent usually has is the false hope the buyer will continue to work with them until an offer is accepted because the buyer and agent have become friends. Many agents do not know how to write up the paperwork so the lender will include the commission in the loan. The buyer does not understand they pay the commission no matter how the paperwork is written since they bring the money to closing. You must enable the agent to sell your house while you keep the situation under control.

Welcome all buyers, with or without an agent.

Tell agents you will not sign a listing agreement of any sort. If their buyer chooses to write an offer, they are to simply place a commission payable to the buyer agency right on the purchase and sale agreement. Tell the agent the percentage of commission you are willing to pay.

Keep in mind the work a buyer's agent will do for you.

➤ Work directly to manage the buyer's needs.

➤ Counsel the buyer to keep them emotionally on track.

➤ Coordinate needed inspections, financing and many other post-offer tasks.

➤ Resolve problems as they arise.

➤ Act as a highly motivated assistant since they do not get paid unless the sale closes.

➤ Be an intermediary between you and the buyer that at times may be able to resolve differences, especially in the case of a personality conflict,

Buyers are accustomed to the seller paying the commission. It does not really matter who pays the commission. All the money comes from the buyer, who pays the price of the home plus closing costs. After all the costs, are paid, including real estate commission, the balance goes to the seller.

It does matter whether the buyer or seller gets the tax deduction of the costs of closing, including commission. You, as the seller get to make this decision. If you need the tax deduction, keep it by paying the commission on your side of the sale.

If your sale is being managed by a relocation service, pay close attention to their rules and use them to your advantage in the negotiation process.

COMMISSIONS

I personally pay a buyer agent, in a FSBO sale of my own properties, a commission of 3–5% depending on the sale price and I do so with a big smile on my face.

As seller, your job is to get the property sold quickly. That means give and take. While pricing your home understand that a certain amount may need to come off the top of the sale for negotiation, repairs or commission.

Calculate those items into your selling budget. If you end up keeping more of the total sales price than you planned, then congratulations.

Real Estate, Real Advice
Exactly How To

Manage

Inspections

4

Home Inspections
Other Inspections

A HOME INSPECTION

A home inspection is a visual examination of the structure
and systems of your house, from foundation to roof. A home
inspection is the equivalent of a physical examination from
your doctor. When problems or symptoms of problems are
found, the inspector will recommend further tests or remedies.

Buyers and sellers both depend on home inspections for
intimate knowledge of the property to help them make smart
decisions.   The inspection summarizes the condition of a
house, points out the need for major repairs and identifies
areas that may need attention in the near future. The
inspection takes approximately three hours. Arrange your
schedule so you can be there, seeing what the inspector
sees. Make sure you completely understand the inspector's
findings.

The inspector will provide you with a report of their findings.
The quality of this report is critical. A one page typed report is
NOT what you want. Hire a home inspector that completes a
detailed multi-page, pre-designed form identifying each facet
of each room.

This report will help you:

> Price your home realistically.

> Find reasonably priced contractors to make repairs
   ahead of time so defects do not cost you hard cash off

the selling price in negotiation and the actual closing happens without delay.

➢ Relieve buyer concerns and suspicions, allowing them to buy your house. Buyers may choose to use your inspection rather than paying for their own.

➢ The professional documentation of a home inspection can limit your liability.

➢ Immediate safety issues may be revealed before your family, agents or potential buyers become injured in your house.

WHO DOES THE HOME INSPECTOR WORK FOR?

The technical answer is the person paying the bill.

The real answer is usually the person that makes the appointment, meets the inspector, works closely during the inspection and hands them the check as soon as the inspection is complete.

Make sure that person is you!

BUYERS WANT A HOME INSPECTION

Major repairs can be major expensive so buyers have learned to use a home inspection as the best available tool to see into the future of that house. A new roof typically costs $4000 - $25,000. A new furnace typically costs $3000 - $10,000. A professional home inspection offers substantial peace of mind on the maintenance and repair that will be needed over the first few years of ownership.

A spotless home offers buyers, inspectors and appraisers the impression of perfect maintenance.

Buying a home is a tough decision. The information learned in a home inspection can justify the buyer's desire to own your house.

GET READY FOR THE HOME INSPECTION

➢ Turn all utilities on.

➢ Clear access to attics, crawl spaces, electric panels, water heaters, furnaces, air conditioners etc.

➢ Unlock doors and have open access to the entire property.

➢ All pets should be removed from the house and yard during the inspection.

➢ Arrange for children to be away during the inspection.

> Have your maintenance file ready for the inspector to review. This information can keep the inspector from making negative assumptions.

> If your house was built with non-typical construction, have construction information ready for the inspector.

> Remove any stored items from bathtubs. The inspector will fill the tub with water and operate the shower.

> If you have a security system, turn it off.

> All appliances included in the sale will be tested by the inspector. Make sure appliances are empty.

A home inspection is a critically important showing. Put the same effort into your preparation that you do for a showing.

HOME INSPECTION REPORT

Clear copies of the Home Inspection Report are kept in the Home Book open to all potential buyers. The accessibility of this report gives buyers a sense of open communication and comfort with the house.

OTHER INSPECTIONS

I recommend at the minimum a home, pest, water, septic and insurance inspection to every buyer and seller client. Inspections give vital information, a sense of security and intimacy with the house and give the seller a work list and reduced liability.

By placing a copy of each inspection in the home book, you may reduce the number of inspections required by the buyer as contingencies on the purchase and sale agreement.

APPRAISAL

An appraisal is typically ordered by the lender to prove the purchase price can be recouped, if the buyer fails to make their loan payments. An appraisal is a property valuation based on the location, improvements and condition in the current market.

ENVIRONMENTAL

Chemicals are found everywhere. They purify drinking water, increase crop production and simplify household chores. Chemicals can be hazardous, if used or released improperly. Hazards can occur during production, storage, transportation, use or disposal. Make sure your house and property are free of all hazardous substances including asbestos.

FEASIBILITY

This is a catch all inspection phrase that allows the buyer to research and inspect every aspect of the location, structures and regulations that will affect the buyer's proposed use for the property. As the seller, remember this is an easy walk away clause that allows the buyer to keep the earnest money. If the buyer wants more than a very few days, charge them a non-refundable fee for the feasibility period.

FIREPLACE, WOOD STOVE AND CHIMNEY

Have a fireplace inspection and cleaning service perform this task while you are in the cleaning phase of staging.

FLOOD SURVEY

Floods are one of the most common hazards in the United States and flood insurance can be very expensive. In certain flood zones, lenders require flood insurance. Flood maps are available at your county offices. These maps offer a general location of the flood zones. Many properties which appear to be in the flood zone prove to be safely outside that zone when you have a flood survey. The surveyor will provide you with an Elevation Certificate.

You will find a link to FEMA and other research resources on www.JuliDoty.com.

GEOLOGICAL HAZARDS

If your land parcel has been cut or filled, you may decide to hire a geotechnical engineer to evaluate the property. If your parcel is on a natural steep slope, talk to an engineering geologist about potential slope stability problems. Many counties have a geologist who has specific data on the stability of land in your area.

GRADING AND DRAINAGE

Most grade caused flooding problems occur in the spring when the ground begins to thaw and spring rain arrives.

The grade is just like a roof on a house. A grade that pitches towards a home can direct water to the home. This can be critical during the winter when the ground is frozen and snow covered. Heavy rains on frozen or saturated ground can quickly cause flooding next to a foundation wall to leak into the basement. This can lead to mold growth within 48 hours. Long term water leaks lead to wood rot in wall framing members and can damage foundations.

1.   Pitch all grades away from a home.

2.   Drain water from gutters into dry wells, french drains or dry creek beds designed into the landscape.

A basement is a hole in the ground. Water fills holes. Keep the house protected by giving water a path to go somewhere else. One great way to do this is by creating a dry creek bed in your landscaping for run off water. It will be beautiful and functional.

MOLD

Molds are fungi. Fungi thrive in moderate temperatures with a cellulose based "food" such as wood products and moisture. Mold spores are common in nature. When they find the appropriate conditions, they multiply, creating colonies of mildew. Ignoring a roof or plumbing leak is a mistake.

Surface molds do little harm to house structures, but they can damage or even destroy delicate cloth or paper materials and there are some health concerns for people with allergies, asthma or depressed immune systems. Wood rot fungi thrive in similar conditions and do significant harm to wood structures, if allowed to propagate. Damp areas should be dried up. If you smell or see mold clean it up and eliminate the moisture source.

PEST

A pest inspection looks for termites, carpenter ants, powder post beetles and carpenter bees, which are all wood destroying organisms. These insects can destroy a house. Hire a home inspector that is certified to do both home and pest inspections, but one that does not offer pest treatment services. You do not want an inspection and treatment company to "find" pests that are not really there in order to sell you expensive treatment services. he pest inspector will also look for wood to earth contact which can attract wood eating pests, dry rot, proper venting and excess moisture.

True Story:

One day during a pest inspection I spoke up and told an employee doing the inspection of my suspicion that his company "found" pests whether they were there or not. He not only confirmed it, but told me his boss instructed his employees "when and where" to "find" a pest problem.

The average charge from that company for pest treatment was $1700.

The employee's honesty was due to the fact it was his last day with that company.

RADON

Radon is a radioactive gas that is a by-product from the decay of naturally occurring uranium deposits in certain underlying rock formations. Very inexpensive tests are available. Contact your local health department.

SEPTIC SYSTEMS

Septic systems are usually not part of a home inspection, but they are a major cost component of the house and should be pumped and inspected prior to purchase. Many bank loans will require this work prior to closing.

Carefully read the wording in the purchase and sale agreement. It may require the septic to be pumped, pumped and inspected or pumped with a certified inspection. Each of the three choices has a very different meaning and cost.

SURVEY

A survey is a certified assessment of the exact location of your property lines. Some states require a certified survey be available to the buyer. Some states do not.

WATER

Water wells should be tested for water quality by the health department or a private lab. This test is important for the health and comfort of the buyer. The buyer's lender may require this water test. Some lenders will require a water quality and water quantity test. Include your well log, water quality test and septic pumping and inspection report in the Home Book.

CRAWL SPACE MOISTURE SOLUTIONS

DOWNSPOUTS

Downspouts need to shed water away from the home (at least 6 feet or more) or to underground pipes that lead away from the home.

IN-GROUND OIL TANKS

If you have an in-ground fuel tank you can remove it or decommission it. In most areas this can be accomplished by removal or by filling the tank with concrete and / or sand slurry. Get your local rules and follow them. Have the soil tested by a lab. Keep your inspection reports available for review.

INSULATION

The paper side of fiberglass insulation should face the heated living space and sit against the sub flooring. When it faces down toward the earth, it has a tendency to trap moisture between the sub floor and the paper, hiding moisture damage.

RAIN GUTTERS

The average roof sheds 1,000 gallons of water during 1 inch of rain. This water will fall along the foundation and find the crawlspace very quickly.   Rain gutters protect the house, foundation and your guests from water damage

SPRINKLERS

Watering plants right next to the house can cause excessive water along the foundation.

SUMP PUMP

Make sure your sump pump is installed at the lowest point in the crawlspace and all areas easily drain to it. The pump should be inspected regularly and function automatically.

A crawlspace is an integral part of your home and should be kept neat, clean and easily accessible. Inspect it often looking for signs of moisture or mildew.

TERRAIN

Make sure that all surface water is directed away from the home. A swale may be necessary, if your home is built on a slope. The foundation can have significant structural damage caused by water along the foundation that freezes in the winter and collapses the foundation inward.

VAPOR BARRIER

Six mil thick poly vapor barrier on the ground of your crawlspace, overlapped and sealed around columns and the walls will help to keep the ground moisture vapors from rising up into your framing.

Remove all debris from your crawl space.

VENTILATION

Open vents in the spring, summer and fall months, even if you must close them during the winter. A crawlspace needs a minimum of 1 square foot of ventilation for every 150 square feet of crawlspace floor area and should be within 3 feet of the corners allowing for cross ventilation.

INSPECTION MANAGEMENT FORM

✓	Inspection	Inspection Company	Paid By Seller	Paid By Buyer
	Access			
	Appraisal			
	Chimney and Fireplace			
	Easements			
	Electrical			
	Feasibility Study			
	Financing Addendum			
	Financial Data			
	Geological Study			
	Hazardous Substance			
	Home Inspection			
	Insurance Availability			
	Investment Potential			
	Neighborhood Review			
	Pest			
	Plumbing			
	Rental History			
	Roof			
	Septic Pump & Inspection			
	Survey of the Property			
	Preliminary Title			
	Underground Tank			
	Water Quantity			
	Water Quality Basic			
	Water Quality Extensive			
	Wood Stove			
	Zoning			

Real Estate, Real Advice
Exactly How To

Stage

For a

Top

Dollar

Sale

5

Staging is Vital to Your Wealth
Answers, Ideas
Staging Forms

Staging is Vital to your Wealth

Today's home buyer is interested in moving into a home that does not require move-in repairs. They don't want to patch and paint the inside or do landscaping on the outside. Buyers pay top dollar for a move-in ready house.

Buyers make an appointment to see your house when they know it is the right size with the right number of bedrooms. What they don't know is if they will like it. Staging the house creates a series of great impressions throughout the home, motivating the buyer to stay. To move in - not move on!

 The ultimate goal of staging your home is to place that house in the best showcase condition, allowing it to sell at the highest possible price in the shortest possible time. When you show off the view, create easy traffic patterns and offer the best curb appeal your odds of that top dollar sale are greatly increased.

Some time ago I listed a newer home that had been on the market for nearly two years! It was very nice. It was very clean! It also held hundreds of collectibles! Possibly thousands! Buyers could not see past the "stuff" to buy the home. I listed the home, had 3 separate staging sessions with the owners and 10 days after listing, we had three offers to choose from.

Some buyers will not even get out of the car because of the poor impression made on the outside.

Every home will sell when it is priced right for the market, the condition and the location. With a staged home, you have the opportunity to ensure your home is priced at it's top potential.

Think about a dress in a store. If the dress is beautifully draped on a graceful mannequin, with lights shining down on glowing fabric, the mannequin's sleek form showing off the perfect dress design…. that dress will sell for top dollar. But take that very same dress, wrinkled and a bit askew on a metal hanger, and you now have a discount in the making!

When buyers look at your house they will see, or at least feel, the flaws. Flaws equal discounts. A buyer looking at your house may not realize the paint is faded or the carpet needs to be cleaned, but the house will feel overpriced.

Let's think back to that dress. Why did you buy the dress on the mannequin? Because you needed a dress or because that beautifully displayed dress caught you *right in the desire.*

Your Home may be the largest asset you ever own.

Selling it may be one of the most important jobs of your life.

STAGE YOUR HOUSE

By showcasing your home's best features, you create a series of great impressions that allow a buyer to connect emotionally while visualizing their life in your house. When a buyer can see themselves living in your house that is the first step to SOLD!

When you put your house up for sale it becomes a product. Just like other commodities, your house must be SEEN in order to SELL. To sell quickly, it must stand out from similar products in the marketplace. Pack, clean, paint and set the stage, make that house ready for the life of the buyer. Staging is a smart investment!

How to do this is simple hard work. Make copies of the inspection forms at the end of this chapter. Get a friend or critical loved one to write down every problem with the house.

You do the same thing. Separately. Is the sidewalk leading to the front door cracked? Does the front door need paint? Does the front door open smoothly? Are the mop boards marred and broken? Does every kitchen cupboard door and drawer close evenly and stay closed? Be picky. Your goal is to make that house sparkling clean, maintenance perfect and desirable.

Think back to that dress in the store.

A woman wants to be her most alluring for an important date. She wears subtle makeup to enhance her natural beauty, the elegant dress she found draped on a graceful mannequin, high heel shoes that accentuate slim ankles and the elegant line of her legs.

She dresses up for her important date to create an image that will spur the imagination into the future.

When getting ready to sell your home, "create an image that will spur the imagination" by offering a visual "stage" where a home buyer can imagine their furniture, their family and their life.

ANSWERS AND IDEAS

BUYERS WOULD RATHER <u>NOT</u> SELECT THE CARPET

Sellers often make the mistake of ignoring certain repair or maintenance items in the hope that "it doesn't really matter."

Imagine yourself walking into a house as a buyer.

While preparing the house for sale, the owner decided, "*it did not make sense to buy new carpet since the buyer would want their own color anyway.*" *He also rebelled against throwing away his stack of car magazines next to his perfectly broken in green recliner.*"

The buyers that are able to imagine how an overly lived in house will look after it is renewed with paint and modern carpet are almost always looking for a price discounted house.

To get top dollar you must present a ready to move in, beautiful home, with no work left to do.

NO, IT IS NOT A GOOD IDEA TO ALLOW A CARPET OR REPAIR ALLOWANCE

You are simply encouraging the buyer to ask for more discounts!

Always price your house for the condition it is in at sale time.

**BUYERS NEED TO FEEL AT HOME,
NOT LIKE GUESTS IN YOUR HOME.**

A personal touch can be too heavy-handed. Make sure your decorating allows "ample space" for buyers to imagine their family, furniture, art work and photographs in that house.

Once you have accomplished this, you are successful at working for the buyer. Yes, I said working <u>for the buyer</u>.

Your job is to see the house from the buyer's eyes and to allow the house to silently answer all the buyer's questions.

Make it easy for the buyer to buy.

….. **Has this house been well taken care of?** Of course, look how clean it is…..

….. **Is there room for my couch in this living room?** Of course, look how open this room is…..

….. **Do you think the seller is hiding anything?** Of course not, all the answers are in the Home Book, right there on the dining room table. This house is an open book. I'm really comfortable here. Maybe we should make an offer on this one….

It is all about using the honesty and reality that allows buyers to see this house as their new home.

GIVE A GREAT FIRST IMPRESSION

1.   Paint the front door and the fence.

2.   Add a concrete patio.

3.   Edge garden areas.

4.   Replace cabinet and door knobs.

5.   Clean the driveway, concrete, front porch and hide the garbage can!

6.   Greet buyers at the front door, hand them a feature sheet and give them privacy to look through the house.

7.   Follow up with a thank you call.

8.   Leave your Home Book open on the dining room table.

9.   Maintain a sparkling clean house.

10.   Set the table for romance.

11.   Arrange fresh flowers in the house.

BUYERS DO NOT CARE ABOUT YOUR PROBLEMS

They do not care why there is junk in the driveway or oil stained concrete. They only care that the mess indicates an opportunity to negotiate harder and pay less.

MAKE SHOWINGS PLEASANT

It is critical to make every showing as pleasant as possible. That means having the whole house ready. You want buyers to feel comfortable and take their time mentally placing their life in your house. Any "turn off" will send them out the door and on to the next house on their list!

WHAT DOES THIS ALL COST?

As little or as much as it makes sense to spend. You generally invest a maximum of 50% of the estimated return and you never invest more than you can afford.

SEE IT ALL FROM THE BUYER'S SIDE

Your goal is to sell the house. To excel at your goal, you must understand the psychology of house selling. Do not make excuses for the things you have not done with the house. Never bring up your hopes and dreams for that house.

To work well with buyers you must turn off your personal defenses. By acting in any possessive manner you actually push the buyer away from that house by reinforcing your ownership. The buyer must "see" their own life in that house. Everything you do must minimize your ownership, and maximize the "at home" feeling of the buyer.

WHAT IS A "GOTTA HAVE IT HOME"?

Many houses on the market are dirty, beat up houses with crummy floor plans. These are not, "Gotta Have It Homes."

A **_Gotta Have It Home_** appeals directly to the "desire". The location works. The cool green landscape offers privacy. The exterior design is original and in perfect condition. The beautiful front door opens to gleaming floors and a perfect floor plan. The décor is dreamy. You just gotta have it!

IMPORTANT HOME STAGING POINTS

1. Decorating with your furniture is the best place to start.

2. Remember that "less is best".

3. Make your home warm and relaxing.

4. Add more value to your home by rearranging each room after you select the appropriate focal point.

5. Involve the entire family.

6. Understand that the job you are doing may be the best paying job you have ever had and with no taxes!

7. You have choices to make. Camouflage the old stuff with pillows, throws or covers. You may be able to get rid of some of the furniture if your house is too full. Furniture is often used as a place to set things that you are too lazy to put away. Store it, donate it, whatever.

DETAILS THAT COUNT

Every day you go to work and, hopefully, you earn a paycheck. Your home has the power to earn a very large paycheck. It may not even have to work very hard.

BRING ON THE ROMANCE. Set a romantic table with your best china. Use the coziness and romance of the fireplace to advantage. Put a pair of wine glasses and a vase of flowers on the coffee table in front of the fire. Set a stage that encourages buyers to imagine how wonderful life would be living in your house.

IF THERE IS SMELL, YOUR HOUSE WON'T SELL. Use simple cleansers like bleach and vinegar to make the home smell clean. Deodorize cat litter and scoop litter twice daily. Put cedar chips inside the closets. Use citrus or vanilla plug-in air fresheners for a consistent gentle, desirable aroma. Do not bake cookies. They create mess and hunger. Hungry buyers go to lunch.

CREATE SPACE. Make sure that all doors, cabinets and drawers open completely without bumping into anything or sticking. Clean out the entry closet. Move oversized furniture to a storage facility. Make sure entrances to all rooms have an open flow. Remove heavy drapes.

MAKE THE MOST OF VIEWS. Disguise unsightly views. Let breezes move your sheer curtains at the window. Make sure the interior is visible from the street. All windows must be crystal clean and clear.

CREATE COUNTER SPACE. Store appliances, dish racks, soap dishes and other every day items inside your tidy cabinets.

AVOID ECCENTRIC DECOR. De-personalize the house by removing dead animal heads or any decorative items that could be offensive.

HOUSEPLANTS MUST FLOURISH, OR DIE. Gangly or excessive house plants detract from the house value.

IMPLEMENT A "KEEP IT CLEAN" PLAN. Everything in the house must stay "presentation ready" at all times.

CURB APPEAL

Curb appeal is crucial. Even if your house is on the small side, if it's well kept, boasting fresh paint, a manicured lawn and beautiful landscaping, you are off to a great start.

IMPROVEMENTS PAY YOU BY INCREASING VALUE

In most cases your home will sell for exactly what it's worth.

The price of your home is set by the market. "Market" is what homes similar in age, quality, size, extras and neighborhood have sold for in the last six months. The average of those sales is the most likely number your home will earn. Your job is to make the market value higher by implementing do-able improvements that increase the **"Gotta Have It"** factor!

Homes are usually chosen from desire. "The neighborhood is perfect! The yard is beautiful. Look at that beautiful paint. Isn't this just the most beautiful house you have ever seen".

Ok. <u>Now the buyer is willing to come inside</u>. Inside they find a spacious home that welcomes their family, their furniture and their life! Your house must continue to <u>silently sell</u> this buyer on the fact that your home is "worth" more than the competition.

<u>Every step you take</u> in preparation must convince the buyer to be the new owner of your house.

Your buyer does not care why there is junk in the driveway or oil stained concrete. (They do not care, **_except_** that mess is a subtle and sometimes not so subtle indication that you need to sell.) Turn off your personal defenses. Do not make excuses for the things you have not done. Assess your reality and do your best.

Write down in detail what you see:

Street view: (note good and bad):
Which access route offers the best impression?
What neighborhood projects are needed?
How does the house look as you drive up?
Why?

With ten being pure honesty and one being a lie, how honest were your answers to the above questions? #_____. If your score was anything less than 10, begin again, at the top.

Get your all your forms on www.JuliDoty.com

Does the house smell?	Yes / No	Of what? _____	
Do pets live outside?	Yes / No		
Is evidence visible?	Yes / No	Smell	Yes/ No
Do pets live inside?	Yes / No		
Is evidence visible?	Yes / No	Smell	Yes/ No

How will you fix it? _____

What is the most attractive feature in this house? _____

What is the worst feature in this house? _____

SET THE STAGE INSPECTION FORM - Page 2

	Flooring	Walls Molding	Window	CeilingLights	Paint	Furniture
Living Room						
Family Room						
Kitchen						
Dining Room						
Laundry						
Mstr Bedrm						
Bedroom 2						
Bedroom 3						
Bedroom 4						
Main Bath						
Master Bath						
Back Porch						
Basement						
Storage						

Complete the above charts with how well each of these aspects of your house looks including what repairs and updating are needed.

	Grass	Land scape	Junk	View	Fences	Ideas
Front Yard						
Back Yard						
Side Yard						
Patio-Deck						
Entrance						
Garage						
Parking						

IMPROVEMENT IDEAS

1. _____
2. _____
3. _____
4. _____
5. _____
6. _____
7. _____
8. _____
9. _____
10. _____
11. _____
12. _____
13. _____
14. _____
15. _____
16. _____
17. _____
18. _____
19. _____
20. _____
21. _____
22. _____
23. _____
24. _____

GET READY

- ❏ Have a yard sale. Many people have enough big toys and junk around that a yard sale will earn enough cash for a small down payment on a new house.
- ❏ Hire help, do it yourself or round up a crew of friends. Whatever it takes, get the job done.
- ❏ Pack up treasures, valuables, collections and all family photos.
- ❏ Lock up guns, cash, jewelry and medications.

_____

_____

_____

_____

_____

_____

_____

_____

_____

_____

_____

_____

_____

_____

_____

_____

_____

_____

_____

_____

_____

_____

MAKE ALL THE REPAIRS

- ❑   Paint gives you the best return for money spent. Use natural calming colors that coordinate with the exterior of the home and the floor coverings and your furniture if the home will be sold occupied.
- ❑   Carpeting must be cleaned or replaced. Giving a "carpet allowance" may be tempting but <u>do not do it</u>. This signals buyer that you are negotiable.
- ❑   Inspect under the sinks throughout the house. Repair all water leaks.
- ❑   Repair the cabinet floors where any damage exists.
- ❑   Check and repair floor damage under hot water tank and toilets.
- ❑   Perfect operation of faucets, toilets and electrical switches and plugs.
- ❑   Secure safety features including stair rails, treads and deck rails.

_____

_____

_____

_____

_____

_____

_____

_____

_____

_____

_____

_____

CLEAN THE <u>ENTIRE</u> HOUSE

- ❏ Clear all unnecessary objects from furniture.
- ❏ Remove piles of newspapers and magazines.
- ❏ Clear kitchen and bathroom counters and cabinets.
- ❏ Remove everything from the refrigerator front.
- ❏ Clean carpets, remove excess throw rugs.
- ❏ Clean drapes - remove if out-dated, leave only blinds or a top treatment.
- ❏ Clean windows – inside and out.
- ❏ Clean the air to remove all cooking, pet, laundry and smoking odors.
- ❏ Use plug-in citrus or vanilla air fresheners.
- ❏ Keep an exceptionally clean home to imply exceptional maintenance.
- ❏ Start early on your move by packing up everything you can now.
- ❏ Pack up the items you do not use daily.
- ❏ Clean out fireplaces and wood stoves.
- ❏ Make sure all closets are neat, clean and organized.
- ❏ Clean and inspect doors and windows.
- ❏ Clean, dust, wash oil and wax everything.

_____

_____

_____

_____

_____

_____

_____

STAGE THE INSIDE OF YOUR HOME

☐ Apply a fresh coat of satin finish paint. Flat paint gives a dry, light-draining look to your room that is not flattering. The exterior color should "flow" into the house. Any time you choose colors get samples of the colors (roofing, exterior paint, exterior trim, wallpaper, kitchen cabinets, flooring) that will not change. Use those colors to coordinate your new paint. It may sound silly, but make sure your color scheme goes well with skin tones so you and your buyer both feel good in the house.

☐ Rearrange or remove some furniture. Paint old furniture for new life.

☐ Leave access and a visual reason to go thru doors.

☐ Create focal points such as a fireplace or view.

☐ In a choice between fireplace and a view as focal point, the view wins.

☐ Hang art at an average person's eye level.

☐ Leave blank wall space for buyers to envision their own art and family photos.

☐ Keep decorations restricted to small groups.

☐ Replace door, cabinet and drawer knobs throughout.

☐ Treat windows with toppers and light fabrics.

☐ The house should look a bit naked.

☐ Play music every day. You never know when a showing may occur.

☐ Keep the house ready to show at all times.

☐ Open window coverings and turn on lights.

☐ Keep garage doors and toilet seats down!

☐ Allow potential buyers privacy to view your home.

☐ Use a consistent color scheme inside and out.

ENTRY

- [ ] Must be especially inviting for buyers.
- [ ] The entry should be clean and well lit with nothing lying around inside or outside.
- [ ] Make the entry feel warm and welcoming.
- [ ] Paint the front door.
- [ ] Pay particular attention to both front and rear entries.
- [ ] Make sure buyers know which door to use.

_____

_____

_____

_____

_____

_____

_____

_____

_____

_____

_____

_____

_____

_____

_____

_____

_____

_____

LIVING ROOM OR GREAT ROOM

❑ Keep furniture at a minimum to allow easy traffic flow and visual space.

❑ Keep only a few decorative items in bookshelves and display cabinets.

❑ Arrange furniture to take advantage of the room's focal point.

❑ Avoid arranging furniture flat to the walls.

❑ Group furniture for a warm, intimate feeling.

❑ Add pillows and throw blankets to accessorize.

❑ If your room allows, have two separate seating areas.

❑ Incorporate console tables, art, sconces, plants, lamps and rugs into the room.

❑ Mirrors can help make a room appear larger.

_____

_____

_____

_____

_____

_____

_____

_____

_____

_____

_____

_____

_____

FAMILY ROOM OR DEN

❑   Make this room inviting but not overly lived in.

❑   Make the room look like a comfortable place to be.

_____

_____

_____

_____

_____

_____

_____

_____

_____

_____

_____

_____

_____

_____

_____

_____

_____

_____

_____

_____

_____

_____

_____

_____

KITCHEN

- ❑ The kitchen is the heart of the home, where families cook, entertain, pay bills, do homework and just hang out. Make the kitchen look its best.
- ❑ Clean the interior and exterior of all appliances. They will be opened!
- ❑ Clean or replace the stove hood filter.
- ❑ Clean cabinet faces. Use a wipe-on wood finish rejuvenating product.
- ❑ Remove clutter and unnecessary items from countertops and clean all countertops and backsplashes thoroughly.
- ❑ Replacing old kitchen faucets.
- ❑ Changing out your hardware. Replacing the hardware on your cabinetry is fairly inexpensive and can totally change the look of the kitchen.
- ❑ Consider updating sink and stove areas with tile, paint or other treatment.
- ❑ Improve the lighting with better bulbs or fixtures.
- ❑ Add artwork to liven up the walls.
- ❑ Window blinds, toppers and other treatments create instant character.
- ❑ Clean vinyl or ceramic floor.
- ❑ Clean grout with bleach products.
- ❑ Place a beautiful centerpiece in the center of your dining room table.

_____

_____

_____

BEDROOMS

❑   Remove all clutter. If you don't need it every day store it, sell it or pitch it!

❑   Arrange furniture to maintain good traffic flow.

_____

_____

_____

_____

_____

_____

_____

_____

_____

_____

_____

_____

_____

_____

_____

_____

_____

_____

_____

_____

_____

_____

BATHROOMS

- [ ] Have all light bulbs working with the highest wattage available and safe for each fixture. Bright is best!
- [ ] Clean and check ceramic tile grout for deterioration.
- [ ] Fix faucet drips.
- [ ] Clean sinks and tubs. Remove rust spots.
- [ ] Re-caulk tubs and sinks. Use a wet/dry caulk applied very carefully with your finger. Smooth it immediately using a wet sponge for a perfect finish.
- [ ] Consider new, color coordinated bathroom linens in natural tones. Do not use harsh colors, especially in small spaces.
- [ ] Remove any evidence of mildew from the shower and bathtub. Spray on products are available that quickly kill the mildew.

_____

_____

_____

_____

_____

_____

_____

_____

_____

_____

_____

_____

BASEMENT

- ❑ If the basement is damp or musty, use a dehumidifier.
- ❑ Give prospective buyers room to move around.
- ❑ Consider painting bare concrete walls white to enhance light and space.

_____

_____

_____

_____

_____

_____

_____

_____

_____

_____

_____

_____

_____

_____

_____

_____

_____

_____

_____

_____

_____

GARAGE

- ☐ Organize tools, remove all debris, pack up the rest.
- ☐ If floor has oil marks, clean it with a commercial cleaning solution.
- ☐ Store packed boxes neatly in a corner of the garage.
- ☐ Miscellaneous
- ☐ Replace the furnace filter.
- ☐ Garbage cans should be kept in an inconspicuous place. Clean your garbage cans to remove smell and grime.
- ☐ Make sure all your faucets are drip-free.
- ☐ Replace any nonfunctioning bulbs in your light fixtures and vanities.
- ☐ Add some final touches, a couple of fresh bouquets of flowers and some nice potted plants in decorative containers. It can do wonders.
- ☐ Remove all excess / aged / dead / sick looking / semi-alive house plants.

_____

_____

_____

_____

_____

_____

_____

_____

_____

_____

_____

KEEP IT CLEAN PROGRAM

- ❑ Vacuum and dust early each morning.
- ❑ Keep dishes done, beds made, laundry picked up.
- ❑ Place bleach tablets in all toilet tanks.
- ❑ Sweep off front and rear porch daily.
- ❑ Shine faucets and chrome daily.
- ❑ Institute an immediate no shoes in the house policy. Everyone, every time! Place a bench or rocker outside the door for comfort.
- ❑ Replace air fresheners as needed.
- ❑ Keep doors and door ways free of handprints.
- ❑ Clean bathrooms weekly. Wipe down the sink and entire tub /shower after every use.
- ❑ Do the windows weekly.

_____

_____

_____

_____

_____

_____

_____

_____

_____

_____

_____

_____

_____

_____

_____

EXTERIOR PREPARATION

❑   Remove any junk or clutter from the yard. This includes tree limbs and leaves, but especially goes for junk cars or parts, lawn tractors, etc.

❑   Power-wash the house exterior. If it needs paint, get competitive bids if you can't do it yourself.

❑   Grass: If possible, reseed any bare areas of the lawn.

❑   Buy a new front door welcome mat.

❑   Embellish your front door area with a nice, big potted plant set off to one side.

❑   Make sure you leave ample space for a comfortable feel at the entrance.

❑   Make sure your street numerals are polished and in place, or, invest in a nice new set that stands out among your neighbors' standard numerals.

❑   Place an arrangement on your front door.

❑   Repair any loose shingles. Bad roofs make buyers uncomfortable.

❑   Check gutters and downspouts to make sure they are clear and functioning properly. Paint them if needed.

❑   Make sure that all exterior lights are operational.

❑   Check gutters and roof for quality and cleanliness.

❑   Wash the siding

❑   Clean, paint or replace the front door.

❑   Sweep and wash the sidewalks, driveways, decks and patios.

❑   Remove cobwebs.

_____

_____

YARD

- ☐ Remove dead or sickly plants.
- ☐ Prune the bushes and trees and keep them from blocking windows.
- ☐ Your yard, decks and patio's are an extension of your interior square footage and need to be inviting.
- ☐ Weed and feed for a healthy green lawn.
- ☐ If you have an unplanted area, remove weeds, till the soil, level the dirt and spread grass seed. Two weeks of heavy water will bring grass and a better chance of selling for more money.
- ☐ Keep the yard mowed.
- ☐ Consider plantings of easy care shrubs in red green and yellow. Cover the ground with landscape material and bark so you have no weeding.
- ☐ Edge plantings and walkways.
- ☐ Fill in holes, repair any damage.
- ☐ Consider concrete or a used brick patio.
- ☐ Prune trees to add privacy, shade and value.
- ☐ Remove all yard debris – including the "good stuff."
- ☐ Edge lawns and gardens.
- ☐ Trim bushes and trees.
- ☐ Wash down sidewalks and driveway.
- ☐ Rake leaves.
- ☐ Clear patios of toys.
- ☐ Trim all shrubbery and plantings.
- ☐ Immediately remove all dog waste.
- ☐ Plant colorful flowers where appropriate.
- ☐ Add bark to gardens and around trees. This is an inexpensive way to refresh the yard.
- ☐ Keep walkways free of mess, ice and snow.

Real Estate, Real Advice
Exactly How To

Price

It Right

6

Price Matters
Exactly How to Set the Price

PRICE MATTERS

Price is the first thing looked at by home buyers. They go to the bank, get pre-qualified and are told by the lender what amount they qualify for. The savvy buyer looks at the qualification number and makes a personal decision on how much they are going to spend based on their financial reality.

> **To earn top dollar bring your house into top condition, then price it right for a top dollar sale.**

Buyers do not look at houses priced out of their range. Those of you who worry about pricing too low and leaving money on the table must stop to consider the number of potential buyers, the time, the effort and the interest payments you will throw away by overpricing.

Even if you were able to find a buyer that would agree to purchase an over-priced house, the bank appraisal process is designed to reject loans on over inflated homes.

Price your house very close to market value, leaving a <u>small</u> amount of room in the price for negotiation.
If you overprice the house with the intention of reducing the price later just "to see what the market will bear", it won't sell and quickly becomes stale on the market. When you later lower the price, a signal is sent to buyers that "problems" may have been discovered.

If the house is under-priced, it will most likely receive low-ball offers. When you need to sell quickly, you must take control and price right for the market, condition and location of that house.

THE LOCAL REAL ESTATE "MARKET" DIRECTLY CONTROLS YOUR PRICE

> **Buyer's market:** many houses competing for a few buyers.

> **Seller's market:** many buyers competing for a few houses.

"Market" is the balance between buyers and sellers.

> **Stable market:** a comfortable balance of buyers and sellers.

Location: You can't get away from this one. If your house is located in a desirable area that is in demand, you will be able to get a higher price than you can for the same house in a less desirable area.

Condition: A house that has been better maintained and shows better, sells for more than one that has poor maintenance and needs work.

Amenities: When a house has extras such as a view, waterfront or beautiful landscaping, it will bring a higher price.

The price you set for your house represents
how honest you are being,
the homework you have done and
your determination to sell or not sell.

EXACTLY HOW TO SET THE PRICE

CMA: COMPARABLE MARKET ANALYSIS

A CMA is a detailed analysis of your local real estate market. It focuses on the sold price of houses comparable to yours. Comparable SOLD houses are:

➢ <u>Sold</u> within the last 6 months

➢ In a very similar neighborhood in the same area (when possible stick only to your own neighborhood)

➢ Approximately the same age

➢ Approximately the same square footage

➢ Of similar style

➢ In similar condition

The average or median price of the sold comparables is the price of your house. You may include value adjustments for superior views, extra land mass or more updating.

Next, look at active comparable listings in your market. Is your house in better or worse shape? Does your house have a great view, and the listings do not? Is your lot smaller than others in your neighborhood?

Homes currently on the market are NOT used to set your value because until they are sold here is no way to know how far down the price may go before they are sold. Houses on the market give you valuable information on competition that you must use to your advantage.

Know your competition and price accordingly.

APPRAISAL

A value is placed on your house by a professional appraiser.

The appraisal will consider location, condition and sale prices of comparable properties.   Most appraisals require three comparable properties be used.

Typically, a lender orders an appraisal to prove the resale value of the house to support a bank loan in case of default.

The lender gives the appraiser the purchase and sale agreement which includes the sale price. This is the amount the appraiser attempts to reach in order to prove the value.

The appraiser researches the market and selects sales that best support the requested value. The selected comparables may be "adjusted" to the specific features of the "subject" property.

In my opinion, this method does not give an accurate picture of what the market will bear on a particular house as the "chosen" comparables may have been inappropriate.

You can hire an appraiser personally and give him the instruction to do a market analysis considering all comparable properties that sold in the prior six months.

HOW TO SET PRICE

Your life style defines the type of sale you choose. Have you treated that house like the investment it is or do you *really* live in it?

The correct price has NOTHING to do with:

1. How much you paid

2. How much you owe

3. Credit card debt

4. What your neighbor or family thinks it is worth.

5. How much you want

Remember!
The price of your home is based solely on the local current real estate market, your location and the condition of your house.

How will you price it?

➢ **Fast Sale**
➢ **As-Is**
➢ **Or Top Dollar**

Every home will sell when priced right for the market, condition and location.

THE RULE OF FULL PRICE

Over-priced real estate goes stagnant on the market. It gets a reputation for "not selling." People suspect you are hiding something. Where there is suspicion, there is fear. When a house invokes fear, offers come in low or not at all.

1.   The seller over prices the home.

2.   The home is shown and finally a low offer is written.

3.   The seller is insulted and angrily rejects the offer with a sense of outrage.

4.   The buyer goes away.

5.   30-60 days later the seller lowers the price.

6.   A new offer is **eventually received and accepted at lower than the original offer.**

RESULTS OF OVER-PRICING

The "new on the market" buyer urgency disappears. Buyers will literally wait until a slower season and see if the house is still on the market.

> I've seen this happen too many times!

As a buyer agent I have advised hundreds of buyers to wait.

The seller continues to make mortgage interest payments, repairs, insurance and taxes on the property. Their costs go up while the profit goes down. The best listing agents refuse over priced listings.

Do not do this to yourself.

WHEN SELLING BY OWNER

The best plan is to follow the list below in order. The correct selling price becomes apparent as the work is completed. You will feel confident pricing your house. It is your choice whether you hire the work done or do it yourself.

- ➢ Have a home inspection that includes a detailed written report.
- ➢ Complete all repairs.
- ➢ Pack, clean and stage.
- ➢ Complete a careful and honest market valuation.

HOME PRICING TOOL

To properly price your house it must be compared to homes SOLD in the last 6 months that be **very similar** in all the following criteria:

Size	Levels	Bedrooms
Style	View	Bathrooms
Location	Square Feet	Amenities
Condition	Neighborhood	Age

You may not compare single level homes to split level, compare frame construction to manufactured homes or compare a new development house to a farm.

You may need to calculate "mean" instead of average which simply allows you to remove the highest and lowest priced sold houses (these may have been outside a realistic range for special reasons) before you add the sold prices together then divide by the total number of sales.

A professional appraiser will look at all the sold comparables and select three that reflect the appraisers target price. Using this method, prices can be skewed away from the true market value. I want you to use and understand all sales.

MARKET VALUE FORM - Page 1				
Description	Subject	Comp 1	Comp 2	Comp 3
Address				
City				
Assessed Value				
Style				
Stories				
Square Feet				
Basement SF				
Bedrooms				
Bathrooms				
Lot Size				
Acres				
Year Built				
Condition				
Garage SF				
Pool				
Outbuildings				
Fencing				
View				
Amenities				
SOLD PRICE				

MARKET VALUE FORM - Page 2

House Condition		Details	Sold Price		Sold Price	Average $ of SOLD Comparable Homes
Excellent		Less than 3 years old		To		
		In perfect repair				
		Spotlessly clean				
Good		Over 3 years old		To		
		Excellent maintenance				
		Spotlessly clean				
Fair		A bit more dated		To		
		Deferred maintenance				
		Wear and tear in places				
Poor		Dated		To		
		Needs maintenance				
		Messy with some debris				
	Number of comparables sold in the last 6 months					
	Average price per square foot					
	Average selling price					
	Average days on the market					

Know Your Competition

	Number currently for sale	
	Average sales price	

What features will make your house stand out from the competition?

Real Estate, Real Advice

Exactly How To

Create Great Ads

7

Advertising Basics
Advertising Methods
Sample Ads & Work Sheets

ADVERTISING BASICS

Quality ads stand out from all the other advertisements and make buyers and buyer agents eager to see your house. Owners compete with professional agents and must do a professional job to capture the best buyer's attention.

You must be proud enough of your house to show off the price and address. Some agents and owners are under the false impression that if they do not include the price or address, then buyers will have to call for the information, allowing the agent to snag that buyer. The false premise of limiting information does not serve sellers.

Pay attention to things that work and don't work in real estate ads.

➤ Never use the words "asking" or "negotiable" with your selling price.

➤ Draw mental pictures with the words you use.

➤ Write every word from the buyer's point of view.

➤ Full sentences are not required, just thoughts and verbal images.

➤ Attempt to fill a need in the buyer's life.

➤ Sloppy ads, just like sloppy house preparation, may hurt your sale price.

WHERE TO ADVERTISE

- ➢   Newspaper

- ➢   Regional Real Estate Magazine

- ➢   Open House Listings

- ➢   Yard Signs with Flyer Box

- ➢   Local Web Sites

- ➢   Bulletin Boards

- ➢   Church

- ➢   Club Meetings

- ➢   Work

- ➢   *Tell everyone you talk to*

As the work to get your house sold progresses, your job is to keep that house perfect, keep your attitude positive and your eyes open. Fix every little fault you see. Be proud of your property.

REACH THE RIGHT BUYER

A house sells when the right buyer knows it is available and is allowed to see it.

Target your marketing efforts toward the right buyer --- then maintain the attitude that every buyer may be the right buyer. You can not judge a person's ability to buy your house from the clothes they wear, the car they drive or from the way they talk.

Target the ideal buyer in your advertising. The target buyer can afford your home and wants to live in it. Other buyers will see your ads, but your chances of a full price, smooth sale increase by reaching out directly, but not exclusively, to the group of buyers looking for a home just like yours.

YOUR ADS MUST SHINE
FOR A TOP DOLLAR SALE

When you want a top dollar sale, present your house with top quality advertising. Top quality ads are not necessarily expensive ads. It is all in the details!

Write your ads from the buyer's point of view. What will the house do for the buyer? What need will the house fill, what comfort will it offer, how will this house improve their life? Make it easy for a buyer to see your house. When they call and want to see it, say sure come on over. When they drive by and see the yard sign and back up, open the door and say, "Hi, come on in." This means your house must stay presentation ready at all times.

➢ Use borders, even around the photo

➢ Use strong simple headlines and an easy to read font

➢ Use only high quality photos – level, no power poles, wires, cars or pets

➢ Use abundant white space

➢ Use very descriptive words

➢ Everything you write must be the truth. Your marketing represents your home. If you lie, it lies. Lies become lawsuits and you do not want to go there.

FOLLOW UP WITH BUYERS

Call every person that looks at your house and thank them. If
the price is adjusted, send out a reduced price feature sheet
to each person on your showing list.

THE ADS YOU WRITE DEFINE VALUE

Take a good look at the next four pages. You will find sample
advertisements that are specifically designed for different
types of sale.

- ➢ **Top Dollar**
- ➢ **For a Fast Sale**
- ➢ **As-Is**
- ➢ **Classified Ads**

TOP DOLLAR SALES
RESULT FROM TOP QUALITY ADS

Perfection **Can Be Yours**

$410,000
4 Bedrooms, 3 Bath, 3 Car Garage, 3400 Square Feet
2100 West Bay Drive, Doty, Washington

Luscious landscaping surrounds a classic brick home built with quality and style in a beautiful neighborhood. View sparkling city lights while treating your guests to a gourmet kitchen meal in the mahogany wainscoted dining room. Open floor plan is gracious with high ceilings and many special features. 12' deep 30x40 in-ground pool. Inspections complete documentation available.   This is a beautiful home.

Call to see anytime 9am-9pm.   (519) 555-3333

FOR A FAST SALE
USE THE TRUTH AS A POWER TOOL.

Motivated Seller

**Sudden Transfer
Offers BIG Promotion.
Must Sell Now!**

Market value:
Est. cost to prepare for a
full price sale:
Fast sale discount: _____
Sale price: **$ 85,000**

Solid 2400 square foot one level home in a great
neighborhood has an amazing city light view and seeks fresh
paint, windows, landscaping and a new family. Be the one.
See at 2324 Jenny Lane, Ariel, New Mexico.
Call now! 444-9999

FOR AN AS-IS SALE
GIVE BUYERS THE NUMBERS

You just want to be done. You are bad at fixing up houses and your dream home is waiting…

We Found Our Mountain Dream Home

Now This Great Home Needs You

Market value:	$100,000
Estimated repair costs for top dollar sale:	5,000
Additional AS-IS discount:	5,000
Priced to sell AS-IS:	**$ 90,000**

Solid 2,400 square foot one level home in a great neighborhood looking for fresh paint, windows, landscaping, kitchen cabinets and a family. Be the one. 784 East Morrow Street, Shelton, ID. Call now. 789.624.1976

Good Classified Ads on the left and not so good in the right column....

Spacious Georgian home awaits you. 3 large bedrooms, includes an exceptional master suite. Bathrooms and the kitchen professionally designed. Spectacular breakfast room overlooks private, park-like yard. Beautiful amenities make this home a must see. Agents welcome.

212 3rd St SE, Quincy
Price: $221,500.
Open Sunday, 12-3.
Call **555-1111** anytime

Big beautiful newer home offers generous gathering space and bedroom privacy. Master suite plus 3 equals 4 bedrooms with 3 big baths in 3,000 sq. feet. Gourmet, kitchen, large yard, great neighborhood near schools. Great condition, ready to move in. Easy to see

300 W Cherry, Baytown.
$245,000
Open House, Sat & Sun 12-3
or call (300) 333-3333

In Town 3 bedroom, 2 bath, cul-de-sac next to school. 888-5555.

Nice House. 3 Bedroom, 1 1/2 B. Nice yard. LBFB, HP/AC, Deck. Big kitchen. Asking $114,500. 555-2222.

Lauderdale 4 Bedroom, 2 bath, built in 1957. $112,000 OBO. 444-3333

YARD AND DIRECTIONAL SIGNS

Yard signs are the most critical advertising you can do.

- ➢ Yard signs should be two sided.

- ➢ Place signs straight and level.

- ➢ Set signs facing traffic.

- ➢ Keep signs sparkling clean

- ➢ Set at driver's eye level.

- ➢ Make sure your signs are highly visible. Prune shrubbery and pull weeds.

- ➢ Never park in front of your signs

DIRECTIONAL SIGNS

Directional signs are placed on the main route you selected for buyers to find your home. They are helpful for open houses and for people quietly researching ads they saw online and in the newspaper.

Directional signs bring buyers to your door that have never heard or read about the house, they simply follow the signs.

INTERIOR HOUSE SIGNS

Small, tastefully prepared and placed signs that briefly point out features help the house sell without your interference.

Do not answer the urge to fill up the white space in your ads and signs. This space is as important as the words. White space in your ads offers the same power presentation that staging your house does for showings.

New Heat Pump 2004

New Septic System and Drain field.
County Inspected and Approved in 2005

Roof new in 2002

FEATURE SHEET

A feature sheet presents the benefits of your house in great detail to potential buyers.

➢ Main Photo (approximately 3 x 4)

➢ At least 2 additional photos minimum size 1 x 1.5

➢ Address

➢ Price

➢ Square footage

➢ Number of Bedrooms

➢ Number of Baths

➢ Year built

➢ Land size

➢ Utility Information

➢ Your phone numbers

➢ Well written description

➢ Special features such as waterfront, swimming pool or nearby attractions

- Clear directions from a major intersection.

- Verify all details. There must be truth in advertising.

- Make every ad you write crisp and clean.

- Use easy to read fonts at 12 point type whenever possible (Arial, 12 point type is what you are reading.)

- Well done feature sheets are a powerful tool in the marketing of your house.

- Your feature sheets should be on bulletin boards, easily accessible by buyers in your home and attached to or near the yard sign allowing easy street side access.

- Put out 25 feature sheets at a time and check the box every morning.

- Include a disclaimer that says you have done your best but do not guarantee any information and suggest the buyer do their own research.

FEATURE SHEET INFORMATION FORM

Use this form as your guide to prepare a useful feature sheet to present to buyers as the answer to their initial questions.

Address							
Const		Frame		Manufactured		Other	
Land							
Size		Acres		Sq. Ft		# Parcels	
Sq Feet		Main Floor		Upstairs		Basement	
Basemen							
t		Daylight SF		Basement SF		Fin / Unfin SF	
Describe		Siding		Heat System		Total # Rooms	
		Roofing		Air Conditioning		View	
		Foundation		Home Style		Waterfront	
		Appliances Included		How Many		Utility Info	
		Stove		Fireplaces		Water	
		Refrigerator		Bedrooms		Electric	
		Dish Washer		Bathrooms		Sewer/Septic	
		Garbage Disposal		Phone Lines		Sprinkler Sys	
		Washer		Deck/Patio		Security Sys	
		Dryer		Outbuildings		Intercom	
Directions							
Description							

Imagine walking into a house and the first thing you see is a classy, open ring binder on the table with a sign that says:

123 Sea Crest Avenue, Seattle, WA

Home Book

FOR YOUR REVIEW

Home Inspection Report
Property Disclosures
County Reports
Utility Reports
Owners Manuals
Seasonal Photographs
Blank Purchase Agreements

That's all the right answers in one place. Buyers tend to react with very pleasant surprise when they see the book, but continue to look at the house. After the showing and when they have interest in buying the house, they come back to the Home Book to have a good look. Having the person choose to sit down in the house is a sign to me of their comfort with this house. I never rush them out.

By providing the Home Book you met rule number one and did not interfere in the buyer's personal thought and viewing process. You offered each buyer all the answers without ever opening your mouth. Your house will feel like an "open book" with nothing to hide.

NEWSPAPER AND MAGAZINE ADS

Research your market by looking through the real estate classified section of the newspaper and home sales magazine to see other ads. Is there a certain week day or certain newspaper section? Is there a regional real estate magazine? Look at these ads. What works? What does not?

In some areas the newspaper is the only local marketing avenue for houses. Others may have a home magazine, radio show or weekly sales newspaper. You want to be where _everybody_ looks.

Each ad you place can and should perform multiple functions. Number one is always to sell the house. You may also advertise an open house schedule or encourage buyer agents.

ONLINE

The internet has revolutionized real estate marketing methods. It has also made it easier for those who wish to sell their home on their own. Several studies show that a huge percentage of home buyers use the internet to perform their own research.

Many newspapers offer a real estate listing web site. These combined FSBO and agent advertising sites can work very well.

Local advertising, including local web sites, is the most important.

ANSWER THE PHONE (YES, REALLY!)

Bad manners, lost messages and the failure to return calls will kill a sale before it is allowed to happen.

"Good (morning, afternoon) evening!" is a lovely way to answer your home phone. The caller will feel great about coming to see your happy house!

Leave a notebook and pen at every phone in the house. Record the name, phone number and information on exactly what each caller says. Even calls you have dealt with. This gives you a permanent record of phone numbers, names, questions and tasks.

Your recorded phone message must be upbeat and interesting. You could say something like, "This is Juli. Yes, you are welcome to see the house today. Please leave me your name and number and I WILL call you back. Thanks."

EXACTLY HOW BUYER AGENCY WORKS

A professional buyer agent and their client sign an agreement that says, in part, if the buyer purchases a home it will be through the buyer agent who will be paid a commission. That agreement may be for a certain amount of time or for a particular house. Some agents will tell you they must list the house in order to write an offer. This is simply not true and in fact forces the agent into dual agency, a position of high risk for the agent, buyer and seller.

WHEN AGENTS CALL TO LIST YOUR HOUSE

You will receive many calls from Real Estate Agents wanting to list your house. They will simply offer their services or may even say they have a buyer, but you must list in order for them to write up the offer.

Have your standard answer prepared.

COMMISSIONS

Real Estate Agents are sensitive about publicly stating commission rates because it is illegal for them "fix" commission rates. As a For Sale By Owner I personally tend to offer a 3-4% Buyer Agent commission, depending upon the price point of the house.

> *"Buyer Agents are welcome to show my home to their clients.*
>
> *I will not sign any type of listing agreement.*
>
> *If your client likes the house, please include a ___ % commission on the purchase and sale agreement.*
>
> *If your offer is accepted, your commission will be paid out of Seller funds at closing."*

TELL EVERYBODY

Tell everyone you talk to that your house is for sale, brag about the best feature and tell the price with pride. Announce it at church, work and club meetings. Keep feature sheets with you at all times to hand out or post on bulletin boards.

ANALYZE YOUR BUYER WORKSHEET

	Fill in with info about your house	Which buyer type fits best?			
		Young Family Moving Up	Empty Nester	First Time Home Buyer	Investor
Square Feet					
Levels					
Home Age					
Number Bedrooms					
Number Bathrooms					
Master Suite					
Condition of Home					
Big Yard					
Sales Price					
Garage / Shop					
Energy Efficient					
Utility Cost					
Children in Area					
Neighborhood Type					
Home Owner Assn					

Place a check mark under the buyer that fits the facts about your house.

If your home were an affordable, 2 story, 3,000 square foot, 4 bedroom, 3 bath home in a newer neighborhood with lots of kids, would an "Empty Nester" be your likely buyer? Of course not. The ideal buyer is a "Young Family Moving Up", unless that home is in poor condition and an "Investor" could buy it at a discount, fix it up and sell at a profit. Every buyer has a motivation. You are in a position to respect and take full use of that motivation.

INITIAL ADVERTISING WORKSHEET

MAIN LINE:

A main line should contain no more than 5 words that create a strong visual image.

CROSS STREET

This is the beginning point for your written directions. Make sure you begin with a well known cross street and direction.

DIRECTIONS

Identify the route that is simple and the <u>most attractive</u>. (Go North on Main from 2nd Street. Drive 2 blocks, turn left on Maple Ave. Go 2 blocks and turn left on Garfield. Pull in the driveway of the beautiful green home on the south west corner.)

LUST FEATURE:

What do your friends and family <u>want</u> most about your house? Fireplace, view, privacy, huge master bedroom…

COMFORT FEATURE:

What makes your house great to live in?

BRAGGING FEATURE

PRIVACY FEATURE

WHAT STANDS OUT

KID FEATURE

COOKING FEATURE

ENTERTAINING FEATURE

WRITE YOUR OWN AD

NOW MAKE IT EVEN BETTER

Real Estate, Real Advice
Exactly How To

Showings
That
Sell

8

How to Sell, Why Others Fail

EQUIPMENT TO HAVE
FOR SHOWINGS

Create a "**Showings Kit**" for buyers. Include a feature sheet and basic floor plan drawing on graph paper. By using graph paper the buyer can either write notes or make quick sketches. Attach the pen to the clip board so it does not get misplaced and frustrate the buyer. Put the camera, flashlight and tape measure inside.

Hand this kit to buyers immediately after your greeting.

➢ Camera: Disposable – **_Give it_** to the interested Buyer

➢ Feature Sheet, Tablet and Pen on Clipboard Case

➢ Pre-printed Floor Plan

➢ Flashlight

➢ Tape Measure

> **Showings are a huge cause of FSBO failures.**

PRE-SHOWING CHECKLIST

☐ Every cleaning task is complete!

☐ Open all drapes and blinds. Turn on all lights.

☐ Make sure the house *smells* good by maintaining active plug-in citrus or vanilla scented air freshener. Use the same scent throughout the house.

☐ Make sure that everything is spotless.

☐ Check the thermostat to make sure that the house is at a comfortable temperature.

☐ Sidewalks clean and ice free.

☐ Remove kids, pets, litter box and extra adults from the house.

☐ Place open Home Book on the dining room table.

☐ Put Buyer Info signs up and looking sharp.

☐ Front door clean and welcoming.

☐ Open the front door for buyers before they reach it.

☐ The longer a showing takes, the more likely it is a great showing. Be patient and do not attempt to hurry the buyer in any way.

WATCH YOUR ATTITUDE

Every person that you talk to, show your house to and that sees your feature sheet is a potential sale, in spite of the facts you are about to read.

- ➤ 96% of the responses to ads and open houses are not real buyers

- ➤ 70% need to sell their house before they can buy

- ➤ 18% live in the neighborhood and are "snooping"

- ➤ 8% are just looking for decorating ideas or shopping

- ➤ Four calls out of 100 are buyers ready and able to buy a home. These 4 prospects look at an average of 21 homes before they buy.

- ➤ Less than 1% of all homes sold are sold at an open house.

- ➤ 3% of all homes sold are from advertising in newspapers and magazines

- ➤ 40% of homes are sold through agent contact

- ➤ 20% are sold through the "For Sale" sign that sits in your front yard

- ➤ 18% of all houses are sold through friends and non-local agents

You must realize that although these statistics are presented in an accurate form, they do not represent your reality.

YOU CAN <u>NOT</u> TELL A SHOPPER FROM A BUYER

Some buyers are determined to look cool and uninterested. Some think it's polite to say they love your home or they might hurt your feelings. Some may insult your home and end up buying it.

Every person who looks at your home is a potential buyer.

Every person will not like your home. Do not judge the ability to purchase your house from a buyer's clothes, car, grammar or behavior.

> **Each person to whom you talk or show your house represents a potential sale.**

Owning your house, in its current condition, is an accomplishment. You have nothing to apologize for. So don't. Apologies are a possessive behavior that hurts your ability to sell.

IT'S SHOWTIME!

Have you ever been to a stage show or circus that begins with the words, *"It's Show Time!"* The sense of anticipation is palpable. The people who look at your house need to feel that same sense of anticipation.

NOW EXCUSE YOURSELF

Do not escort the buyer. Wait either in the front yard or the front room. Be busy working on your move in some way.

Why those locations? You will be available there to thank the buyer on their way out and answer any questions they may have. **DO NOT TALK!**

Answer questions. Be gentle and quiet. <u>Never</u> tell stories about your kids growing up in the house. Your hopes, dreams, and plans for that house are immaterial and actually work against you.

> "Welcome.
>
> Feel free to open, snoop, flush. Do whatever you need to do.
>
> This house may become your new home."

The buyer must be able to focus on their own dreams and plans as they walk through the beautifully staged house. Will my furniture fit? Which bedrooms are best for the kids? Can we afford to remodel the kitchen? Let's remove that huge tree in front, it hides the house!

You must keep your ownership and life out of the way so buyers can dream their way into actually buying the house.

➤ Buyers who look uninterested can turn into "The Buyer"

➤ Say please and thank you

➢   Have pride, not ownership, in your product

SECOND SHOWING

A second showing means at least one of the people in the group really likes the house. At this point give the buyers extra space, but be available for questions.

RECOGNIZE YOUR OWN
Failure Behaviors...

1. **CHATTING.** The buyer is there to visit the house, not you.

2. **FOLLOWING THE BUYER AROUND LIKE A KID SUSPECTED OF STEALING.** The buyer will <u>run</u> away from your uncomfortable house.

3. **TELLING THE BUYER YOUR PLANS & DREAMS FOR YOUR HOUSE.** You have just reinforced your home ownership. The buyer can not create dreams of their future when you keep sharing yours.

4. **GETTING TECHNICAL.** Most buyers do not care about the location of the water shut off valve the first time through the house. Your job as a FSBO is to be available but completely unobtrusive. The buyer will ask questions when they are ready. Make sure you answer the questions honestly, but without extra conversation. Guide the buyer to the home book for a map of the important mechanical features.

5. **DO NOT TELL BUYERS MORE THAN THEY ASK.** Buyers ask questions when they are ready to hear the answers.

Real Estate, Real Advice
Exactly How To

The World's Greatest Open House

9

All the Details

OPEN HOUSE DETAILS

Open houses require preparation, energy and enthusiasm, at a time when you are exhausted from staging your house. The financial rewards of a top dollar sale make it all worth it.

Buyers learn to power shop open houses. They do not need to schedule an appointment and they do not have to deal with an agent when they would rather not. Attending open houses is within their control and <u>easy</u>.

Decisive buyers do not want to chat, be directed around the house or have inane conversations. They want to find their new home and if your house is not right, they will move on. Although this may seem rude to you at first, get used to it. It is an effective and professional way to sell your house by owner.

THE PLAN

EXTRA PEOPLE AND PETS LEAVE FOR SHOWINGS

➢ Children may be underfoot or capture the buyer's attention.

➢ Children blurt out things you may prefer a buyer not hear.

➢ Children are a strong visual reminder that this is THEIR HOME. This knowledge breaks buyer's ability to visualize your house as their home. You must take your family out of the buyer's decision making process by never letting them attend showings, by removing family photographs or other reminders of the current occupants.

➢ Extra people of all ages should be gone during every showing.

ANTICIPATE BUYER QUESTIONS
IN YOUR WELL PREPARED HOME BOOK

➢ Know how far it is to the schools in your district.

➢ Know the distance to the post office and supermarket.

➢ How close is public transportation?

➢ Where are medical facilities located?

OPEN HOUSE PREPARATIONS

For an open house scheduled to start at noon, have your open house signs in place by 11:45. People tend to begin arriving as soon as they see the first sign or as soon as the appointed hour strikes, whichever comes first.

How many times have you seen a yard sale ad that emphatically states, "No early sales!" How dumb is that? When you have a product to sell and a buyer arrives, be open for business! Never keep your public waiting.

It takes two people to properly work an open house. Station one near the <u>open</u> front door greeting buyers, directing them toward the buyer sign-in sheets. The second open house host spends their time quietly wandering around the house and yard, answering questions when asked, but otherwise being unobtrusive. The wandering presence offers home security, and they are able answer whatever questions have popped up in the buyer's mind. This gives the buyer a sense that the house may just be the answer they seek.

After they sign in, hand <u>every</u> attendee a feature sheet (*yes*, both husband and wife and even the kids. You have just made the kids feel happy and important in that house).

Greet each buyer with, "Make yourself at home. Feel free to open cupboards and closets. Look through the Home Book for detailed information about the house and property. It is on the dining room table. I am Juli. Ken and I are here to answer any questions you may have. Enjoy yourself."

Although you may feel more successful if you have many attendees at your open house, it only takes one buyer to make the sale.

Besides obvious buyers, you will play host to neighbors, friends that drop by in support of you, people looking for decorating ideas and a few who simply like looking at homes. All of these extras are OK. If you try to weed them out you will create an uncomfortable atmosphere that drives off real buyers. Non-buyers have family and friends that may be in the market for a new house.

The privacy you allow open house visitors gives them the opportunity to envision their life in your house. When you over manage showings, most buyers will just want to get away from you(r house).

Always use the same air freshener scent throughout the house. If you can not get citrus, use vanilla. Both these scents make people feel a bit of longing. Not hunger. This feeling of longing can be transferred to the house, instead of the stomach. Do not serve snacks. Snacks are messy and require polite conversation. Conversations between strangers turn to families, which is a very bad idea.

Make sure medication, cash, weapons and collectibles are securely put away during the entire sales process.

Thank every attendee for coming and make sure they have a number to call in case they would like a second showing.

Follow up on every Open House visitor with a phone call

thanking them for attending and asking if they have any questions or comments. Some will tell you what they did not like about your house. Buck up, you need to hear this. It is one person's opinion. They may also be right.

ENCOURAGE YOUR NEIGHBORS TO ATTEND

Advertise in the real estate section of your local paper, but make a special effort to tell the neighborhood.

Neighbors are the best promoters of living in the area and some of their friends are possible buyers. Put flyers out for blocks around.

YOU'RE INVITED TO AN OPEN HOUSE

We've loved being your neighbors, but sadly, we will be moving soon. We are selling our home (asking $299,500) and will hold it open this Sunday from noon to 3 pm.

We would love to have you come by. Our home might be perfect for a friend or relative of yours! See you there!

Jason and Becky Grayson
3925 Walker Way, Wenatchee

BE PREPARED TO LISTEN
WHEN A BUYER REALLY INSISTS ON TALKING

Listen closely and keep the conversation where it needs to be. Ask questions that go back to the house. Draw out the buyer's needs such as entertaining at home, which means emphasizing the living-dining area; doing lots of cooking, which means a serviceable, bright and cheery kitchen; or gardening. These conversations can help you frame a subtle sales pitch geared toward the buyer's interests and practical needs. If, for example, the buyer mentions that he took a recent bicycle trip, mention the nearby bike paths. If he says that bread is his favorite food, point out that there are three bakeries in the area.

When you listen you will hear comments that can help you get your house all the way to SOLD. If buyers want to know school district boundaries, they obviously have or are planning to have children. Not only should you talk about the school district, but mention other child-related attractions, such as a nearby park or day care center, light traffic on the streets or other children in the neighborhood.

DON'T OVERWHELM BUYERS

Some people look at hundreds of homes, a few at just one. Some people go to open houses as a hobby and don't ever really plan to buy one. All these people come to look at your house. Please do not attempt to entertain them.

Great staging will silently show off the features the buyer is interested. Do not go overboard praising the house.

DO NOT GIVE OUT PERSONAL INFORMATION

Personal information may be used against you in negotiating a sales price or contract.

<u>SEE</u> THE HOUSE AS IF YOU WERE BUYING IT

THINK ABOUT: Probable down payment, closing costs and monthly costs of ownership, including taxes, insurance, utility costs and needed maintenance.

CONSIDER BOTH SIDES: Neighborhood conveniences and services such as school district, parks, shopping and transportation.

INVESTIGATE: Zoning ordinances, including restrictions about adding on to a house.

KEEP YOUR SENSE OF HUMOR

Many buyers look at houses the way they look at used cars -- they pick on every flaw they can find. Your job is to take all comments in stride. This "exaggerate the flaws" behavior is a common negotiating style. Sometimes it is just bad manners, but it is not your problem. Those picky, negative shoppers have often surprised me and purchased the house.

OPEN HOUSE

Make sure you have fully prepared the house with staging that included removal of photos, valuables, guns, drugs and collections.

Prepare a special open house for your entire neighborhood. Turn on all the lights, set the table "for romance" and show your neighborhood just how perfect this house would be for their friends and family on the move.

Check your area for typical open house schedules. That is when you do them.   Avoid times when most of your buyers will be otherwise occupied. If there is no standard timing, I suggest the times below:

➢   Saturday and Sunday Hours: noon to 3

➢   Thursday or Friday Hours: 4pm to 7pm

LAST MINUTE OPEN HOUSE PREPARATION

> A spotlessly clean home is essential. Dirt will turn off a buyer faster than anything.

> Mow your lawn. Put away all toys and yard tools.

> Turning on the sprinklers for 30 minutes make the lawn sparkle.

> Even in the daytime turn on the lights to add shine.

> Open all curtains

> Send your pets away with the kids. Animals turn off the multitude of allergic people.

> Put colorful fresh flowers in principal rooms.

> Add fresh towels and new guest soaps to every bath.

> Set the table with pretty dishes and candles.

> Buy a fresh doormat.

> Put away kitchen appliances and personal bathroom items to give the illusion of more counter space.

> Lay a fire in the fireplace. If it's cold outside, light it.

> Attach balloons to draw special attention to your yard and directional signs.

> It is OK to ask guests to remove their shoes or put on shoe covers. I leave mine outside the door as encouragement.

OPEN HOUSE TOOLS

GUEST SIGN-IN SHEET: Get the name and address of everyone who attends. Make notes, jot down impressions and comments and make sure you can get back to people who show interest. This becomes especially important if you lower your price or change terms later on.

8-1/2 X 11 INCH FLYERS: Fact-sheets describing your home, listing your price and how to reach you. Every guest should leave with an 8 1/2 x 11 inch real estate flyer.

OPEN HOUSE KICK OFF TO YOUR SALE

A huge percent of homes are purchased by friends and relatives of people who already live or work in the neighborhood. Make sure everyone who attends the open house leaves with a flyer that lists your price, phone number and describes the property.

Hold your open house on a Saturday or Sunday afternoon. Sundays are better and noon - 3 PM is the best time. Check the calendar to make sure your open house is not competing with major national or local events.

OPEN HOUSE SECURITY

➢ Work in teams. Wander through the house saying just a word or two to people and move on. You don't want to infringe on their fantasizing about owning that house, but you do want to be a gentle presence able to answer a question that doubles as security.

➢ Have a sign in book for guests and use it.

➢ Create an emergency code. The security code in my real estate office was a direct request in person or on the phone for the "red file." This meant I needed immediate police support.

➢ Open house guests must be comfortable enough to open closets and cabinets.

BE CAUTIOUS WITH ANYONE WHO

➢ Is preoccupied with art, electronics, medicine cabinets (drugs) or other contents of a house and examines windows, locks or alarm systems.

➢ Exhibits body language that suggests something is wrong (dilated eyes, labored breathing, nervous movement, or inappropriate laughter).

Please complete this page and then make yourself at home!

Inside you will find

Our Home Book on the Table with all the Details

Feature Sheets

Plat Map

Utilities

Covenants, Conditions & Restrictions

Welcome

Name _____

Address _____

Phone _____

Email _____

Buyer Agent _____

I stopped by today because _____

_____

_____

_____

I would like a second showing on ___/___/___ at __am/pm.

I need information about _____

_____

WELCOME FORM – SIDE 2

Buyer purchasing alone?   Y / N   Who _____

Buyer working with an agent?   Y / N. Who _____

Buyer pre-approved?   Y / N. By _____

BUYER LIKED

BUYER REQUESTS TO FULFILL

BUYER DID NOT LIKE

IMPROVE FOR NEXT SHOWING

FOLLOW-UP PLAN

TO REMEMBER THIS BUYER

THANK YOU CALL _____/_____/_____ _____

Keep this 2-sided sheet on an attractive clipboard with attached pens. Have a number of sheets on each clipboard. The front side is for the buyer. Use the back for your personal notes and tracking.

Real Estate, Real Advice
Exactly How To

Ethics

Real

Estate

Reality

10

Knowledge is Protection

SELLERS HAVE A LOT TO LOSE

Both sides of a real estate transaction can lose money, but typically the seller loses cash, buyers lose opportunity.

In my opinion there are three reasons why consumer protection is so poor in real estate:

1 _Real Estate is a big business_. Selling prices are big. Commissions are big. Big money creates big greed.

2 _The real estate industry is 'controlled' by real estate agents._

3 _Consumers lack knowledge_. Many never know how much they lost due to an inexperienced or unscrupulous agent.

Agents face frequent opportunities to make **self serving decisions** which can often be rationalized within the rules of agency.

Real Estate is valuable.

Valuable commodities often reveal the honesty and integrity of the people involved.

Put everything in writing and have every person sign and date every document.

Treat each signing, showing, and negotiation as an emergency.

Politely require documentation of research and "facts."

Do every job now. Put off nothing for later.

ADVERTISING COST REPAYMENT

Many listing agreements state that unsold or canceled listings can result in a direct advertising charge made to the unsuccessful seller. When preparing this bill, some agents will include the full cost of every ad on which your house appeared – even though the ad may have been shared by many other houses.

Some advertising done by your listing agent will be designed to sell your house, and some ads are designed to get new seller and buyer clients for the agent.

Agents will sometimes team up with a lender to advertise their listings. The lender actually pays the advertising cost so the agent will promote the lender on every listing.

Make sure you go to your agent's office and request a copy of every bill, the ad it is for and a copy of the actual check it was paid with.

APATHY

The treatment given to many home buyers is often flippant and casual. Many buyers are stunned at the almost complete lack of interest shown by real estate agents when asked to see a house.

BETRAYAL OF CONFIDENCE

Some agents are quick to betray the confidence of sellers. If the seller is ill, going through a divorce or has financial problems, this highly sensitive information is often given to buyers. The personal details of the seller client's life should never be revealed without the seller's permission.

UNTRUTHS

Potential listing agents will escalate a proposed selling price in order to obtain the listing. The highest proposed listing price does not make the best agent. Believe the statistics you see in a properly done market valuation.

INVESTMENT ADVICE

Advice from agents about the investment potential of a house or piece of property is often wrong. Agents are paid only when they make a sale so the entire industry has been trained to encourage a purchase even when it may not be the best thing for the buyer.

Mortgaging your home in order to purchase investment real estate is risky and stressful. The risk is high in spite of the fact that many real estate agents will tell you it is the right thing to do. Make sure you always have at least two ways to pay back the debt of investment real estate.

OVER BORROWING

Homebuyers are often encouraged to pay more than they can afford. A future increase in interest rates will cause these over extended borrowers to lose their home and their credit rating. Pay only as much for your home as you are comfortable paying.

READ EVERYTHING!

If you "must" sign it today or lose it, then lose it. My Grandma Muriel always said, "Nothing ever goes out of my life except to make room for something better." I really believe that high pressure is not the right atmosphere for important decisions.

When an agent states they are not allowed to leave the documents with you overnight for reading and consideration, send him away, never to return. That is either a lie or the regulation of a company I would personally not work with.

➢ Insist on having your closing documents overnight for review before signing.
➢ Understand the purchase and sale agreement and your house financing so well you can make fast decisions when you receive an offer.
➢ Be decisive, but take the time you need to make educated decisions.

UP-FRONT INSPECTION EXPENSE

Expensive services are often recommended to Sellers that may or may not make them money. Make sure your agent gives you a written analysis that convinces you of the need to spend money. The expenses I most commonly recommend to my clients are a preliminary title review ($50) and a home inspection ($400). It is in your best interest to discover, and resolve, problems before they become an emergency.

YOUR AGENT CAN BE A HERO,
OR LESS THAN ZERO

If you decide somewhere during the FSBO process to list with an agent, I want you armed for success. The lesson in the following example is powerful. The possibility of a similar situation happening to you is strong.

Real estate agents have a professional association that has devised a Code of Ethics mandated to keep the profession strong, ethical and always working in the best interest of the client. But the other side of the story is that opportunity knocks loudly for the opportunistic real estate agent.

Imagine a listing agent receiving 3 different offers for a single listing. Which one should the agent encourage the seller to accept? The best offer, right? Let's inspect the numbers.

Property listed a $100,000 with a 6% Commission
LA = Listing Agent   BA = Buyers Agent   DA = Dual Agent

Look at the top half of the following chart. That is the point where most transactions reach mutual acceptance, but that is not good enough! Can you imagine what happens to these numbers on a higher dollar transaction where the loss to the seller might easily be $25,000 or more? Don't let that be you.

LET'S FOLLOW THE MONEY
WITH THE FIRST ROUND OF OFFERS

Buyer 1: $100,000 x 6% = $6,000 commission.
Commission split equally between listing and buyer agent

Buyer 2: $98,000 x 6% = $5,880 commission.
Commission split equally between listing and buyer agent
Buyer 3: $100,500 x 6% = $6,030 commission.
This is entirely paid to the listing agent as she listed the
property with the seller and wrote the offer for the buyer.

The obvious answer is **NOT** to take the listing agent's offer at
$500 over full price.

This is an ideal opportunity for negotiation. With 3 offers the
house is clearly desirable. Counter-offers should be made to
each of the 3 buyers. My favorite method for countering
multiple buyers is to ask for the highest and best offer over a
specified amount. Tell all agents, in writing, that you will
accept the highest and best offer over $100,500. Include any
other critical terms. Some buyers will cooperate, some may
be insulted and some may stand their ground. The seller
typically ends up with the strongest buyer and the transaction
was honest to all parties.

With the listing agent offer only $500 over the highest offer
you must wonder if the listing agent got the highest offer
possible or was working just barely hard enough to earn the
entire commission. If a listing agent did not suggest further
negotiation we have serious ethical concern. The seller is in
a strong position with 3 offers and the listing agent may be

working harder for the commission than to get the highest and best offer for the seller.

When buyer agents do not receive the same full disclosure that the buyer working with the listing agent received, then neither the seller, who could have received a higher price nor the other potential buyers, who could have offered more and got the house, were treated honestly.

Home Listed at $100,000	Buyer Agent 1 Offer 1	Buyer Agent 2 Offer 2	Listing Agent & Buyer Agent = Dual Agent Offer 3
Initial Offer Amounts	$100,000	$98,000	$100,500
Listing Agent Commission	$3,000	$2,940	$6,030
Buyer Agent Commission	$3,000	$2,940	$0
Net Proceeds to Seller	**$94,000**	**$92,120**	**$94,470**

When the seller requests the highest & best offer from each buyer look below to see what happens to the sellers net – and to the winning offer!

Highest and Best Offers	$105,000	$98,000	$103,000
Listing Agent Commission	$3,150	$2,940	$6,180
Buyer Agent Commission	$3,150	$2,940	$0
NEW! Net Proceeds to Seller	**$98,700**	**$92,120**	**$96,820**

The seller made an extra $4,230 by asking for highest and best offers from all buyers. Just imagine the increase in profit on today's average price home!

The second half of the chart above shows the typical responses that may have come back to the seller if the buyers had been given the opportunity to come back with their highest and best offer.

In this simple, low dollar example, the listing agent's greed (or lack of expertise) cost the seller $4,320. On a $500,000 transaction, more in line with today's real estate pricing, that equates to a $21,150 loss to the seller.

Buyers 2 and 3 have now been treated fairly and in fact, buyer 1 will likely be the offer accepted by the seller.

Listing agents can and do manipulate offers for greed.

By cooperating with buyer agents, negotiating fairly and working hard, everyone wins. Earning 50 percent of the commission on many sales is far more profitable for the intelligent listing agent than keeping 100 percent of the commission.

Excellent agents know that supporting buyer agents in the sale of their listings is very good business.

As a seller, you might be aware some buyer agents do not show properties listed with difficult listing agents. Some agents do not show FSBO properties. Some do. Paying a commission to an agent who shows your home to a buyer and brings the transaction to closing is a win for everyone.

Real Estate, Real Advice
Exactly How To

Paperwork

11

Common Documentation
Sale Tracking

COMMON DOCUMENTATION

WHAT IS IN THE PURCHASE AND SALE AGREEMENT?

There will be state requirements and regional practices that design the forms used in your state. Most real estate contracts contain the following:

1.   **What**: Street address, city, state, zip code, assessors tax parcel number and the legal description of the property.

2.   **How much:** Selling price.

3.   **Finance contingency:** Subject to obtaining a loan (if applicable) and the specifics of the loan including amount, rate and term. This contingency will also define the number of days the buyer has to apply for financing.

4.   **Earnest Money Deposit:** the detail includes how much money accompanies the contract, who will hold the money and how it will be dispersed if the contract goes into default.

5.   **Closing:** When, where and managed by whom.

6.   **Included:** What is and is not included in the purchase

7.   **Home inspection:** If there will be a home inspection, who pays for it, when is the deadline for completion and approval and who will get copies of the home inspection report.

8.   **Warranties:** Included with the house and description of the warranty.

9.   **Well and septic:** If applicable, they must be tested according to the terms of the agreement (and pass).

10. **Termite and pest inspection:** Who will pay for the inspection, and who will pay for any required repairs.

11. **Possession date:** Defines when the buyer may take possession of the house. This can be before, at or after closing.

12. **Acceptance:** How long the sellers have to respond to the offer with either acceptance, rejection or a counter-offer.

13. **Arbitration:** Provisions for arbitration of disputes.

14. **Property disclosures.**

PRE-SALE DISCLOSURE

Keep the original disclosure form in your personal house file. Place at least 5 sets of the completed home disclosure form in the home book so you can hand a complete set to interested buyers. Make sure you obtain the buyers signature on your copy at the same time as the purchase and sale agreement signatures. Many disclosures are mandated by law and these signatures prove you made the required disclosures.

DISCLOSURE FORMS

Tell all the material facts you know about the home. Answer questions honestly. Buyers deserve to know the truth.

Honesty is absolutely the best policy.

LEAD BASED PAINT: Houses constructed prior to 1978 may have lead based paint. You need to tell what you know. In most cases, home owners do not really know anything as they have not tested and did not own the home "back then." That is OK, just tell the truth.

MOLD: Read the section on mold in inspections. Fix the problems and then disclose you had and fixed the problem.

PRE-SALE RESEARCH

Have your name, address and tax parcel number available when you contact your city, county, state and federal offices to obtain the following information.

- ➢ Assessor records (county)

- ➢ Auditor records (county)

- ➢ Treasurer records (county)

- ➢ Utility expense history (utility offices)

- ➢ Septic system as-built (city or county)

- ➢ Water well log (Department of Ecology)

- ➢ Irrigation right documentation (water district or Department of Ecology)

- ➢ Home blueprints (your files or local building and planning office)

- ➢ Manuals for appliances (your files or online)

- ➢ Homeowner association bylaws and regulations

- ➢ Covenants and conditions (your files, home owner association or auditors office)

- ➢ Shared road agreements (these should be recorded with the auditors office)

- ➢ Easements of record (these should be recorded with the auditors office)

- ➢ Zoning (city or county)

PURCHASE AND SALE AGREEMENT

Your state may have a multitude of required forms. You should discuss with your attorney or licensed escrow agent the forms you will need for your region.

Completely understand your region's usual purchase and sale agreement forms before you ever receive an offer.

- Purchase and Sale Agreement

- Financing Addendum

- Inspection Addendum

- Insurance Addendum

- Hazardous Waste Addendum

- General Addendum

- Private Septic Addendum

- Private Well Addendum

- Feasibility Addendum

- 1031 Exchange

Real estate forms for every state are available at www.JuliDoty.com

IDENTIFY YOUR TEAM

Who will do the actual work? Who can you count on for expert information?

➢ Title Company: prepares preliminary title inspection and a policy of title insurance.

➢ Escrow Company: collects earnest money and prepares documents for the actual closing. Attorney: some states require an attorney perform the closing work.

➢ Attorney

➢ County Offices

CONTINGENCIES

A contingency is a term written in to the purchase and sale agreement that defines an event which must occur before a contract is binding.

A common example is the financing contingency which effectively states a buyer agrees to buy your house unless the bank refuses to approve financing acceptable to the buyer. Should the financing be refused, then the seller has agreed to return the buyer's earnest money.

It matters greatly how every form is filled out. It was very common in my real estate practice to receive offers written by agents that did not protect their buyer by properly completing ALL the paperwork

Read every document carefully. You must understand what it says and what it does not say. You may discover, as I did, that agents do not always understand the forms themselves.

COMMON COUNTER OFFER ITEMS

When you counter offer on any term in the purchase and sale agreement submitted to you, <u>you hand the buyer a walk away free card</u>.

When an offer is close, strongly consider accepting the offer as is. If you have an easy relationship with the buyer, ask them openly about changing minor items such as closing date or what is included in the sale. Get their agreement right then and as always, all parties must initial and date every change

PURCHASE PRICE

The amount at which buyer and seller agree to complete the sale.

FINANCING TERMS

The length of time a buyer has to prove financing, how much they will invest in a down payment, how much they need to borrow and the terms at which the buyer will complete the loan.

CLOSING DATE

From the seller's side, sooner is much better for closing. Buyers die, get divorced, get fired…. You want the sale done as soon as possible.

POSSESSION DATE

This is the date when the buyer can assume possession of the house. It can be before, at or after closing. Allowing the buyer early occupancy can cause a number of problems including liability, buyer remorse and damage. If the furnace breaks, who is responsible to fix it? If there is a major water leak, who is responsible?

My Advice

If you feel you must give early occupancy, require a written agreement on repairs and liability. Also require a substantial non-refundable earnest money be delivered to you personally prior to any early occupancy.

INCLUDED ITEMS

Everything attached to the land and improvements is usually included in the sale automatically. This includes light fixtures, toilets, built in appliances, etc. If the buyer is asking for something extra it must be included in the purchase and sale agreement or contracted on a separate document. If you are going to leave debris or other personal items you should include details of how, where, and how much, etc.

CLOSING

Your state will have its own standards of practice. Laws vary dramatically from state to state. Call your title, escrow, closing company or attorney to make sure you have met all your personal needs and legal requirements. Ask questions of your closing officer.

Request the closing documents a day before you sign them. Go through them carefully and make sure you understand the paperwork and that the terms of your purchase and sale are met.

Some of the financial forms can be difficult to understand. Although I have certainly found mistakes, it is more common to have confusion caused by the debits, credits, legalese and small print.

SALE TRACKING FORM

Complete this form to have the details of your sale in one place. Give a copy to all parties for an organized wonderful transaction.

THE PROPERTY

Property Address	
Parcel Number(s)	
Selling Agent Name	
Selling Agency	
Selling Commission	%

MANUFACTURED ONLY

VIN if Manufac.		Is Title Eliminated	
Make		Year of Manufacture	

OTHER CONTACT INFORMATION

Mortgage Co.		Title Co	
Loan #		Loan #	
Phone		Phone	
Fax		Fax	
eMail		eMail	
Mortgage Co.		Escrow	
Loan #		Loan #	
Phone		Phone	
Fax		Fax	
eMail		eMail	
Insurance Co.		Renter	
Agent		Phone	
Phone		Mo rent	
Fax		Paid To	
eMail		Deposit	

ALL ABOUT THE BUYERS

Buyer Name	Mailing Address	Contact Numbers	
		Home	
		Cell	
		Work	
		Fax	
		Email	
		SSN	
Spouse or Other	Mailing Address	Home	
		Cell	
		Work	
		Fax	
		eMail	

ALL ABOUT THE SELLERS

Seller Name	Mailing Address	Contact Numbers	
		Home	Cell
		Work	Fax
		eMail	SSN
Spouse or Other	Mailing Address	Home	Cell
		Cell	Fax
		Work	SSN
		Fax	
		eMail	

RENTAL AND TENANT INFORMATION

Name		Deposit Amount	
Rent Amount		Deposit Held At	
Rent Due Date		Rent Paid Thru	

Real Estate, Real Advice
Exactly How To

Understand

Offers

12

Understand Offers

Treat every offer and negotiation as an emergency.

If the buyer wants to hold a property off the market for an extended period of time prior to closing, the buyer should pay a non-refundable fee for that privilege. For instance: A seller places his house on the market in a HOT market. A buyer offers to buy, at full price, with the standard financing and inspection contingencies with the purchase to close in 4 months. This is risky for the seller. Two months later the market has cooled, prices are down and the buyer suddenly loses their job. The financing fails and the house, is not sold.

Due to standard contingencies of financing and inspections the seller must return the earnest money to the buyer. The buyer had protection, but the seller did not. The seller has missed the best market and may have to accept a lower price.

A better solution may have been for the buyer to go ahead and close but rent back to the seller for 4 months.

OFFERS

Acceptance of an offer does not mean your house is sold. An offer is simply an offer. It must be negotiated into terms that work for all parties. The buyer must be approved by the lender, the house must be approved by the appraiser and the appraisal must be approved by the lender. Hopefully no one will die and high tide does not end up in the living room before closing. Things happen. Be prepared to deal with problems, renegotiate or even start over.

BACK UP OFFERS

Once you have an offer, continue to show the house and accept backup offers. A back up offer is just that, an offer received and accepted under the written condition that if the first position offer fails to close, then buyer two is ready and waiting in the wings. Terms accepted on the first offer have no effect on offer two.

MULITPLE OFFERS

All offers should be treated equally, no matter who writes the offer or when it was written. In Washington state there is no priority given to the order received. The seller has the right to work with any or all offers they receive in the order of their choice or all at the same time.

VERBAL OFFERS

Never get involved in verbal offers. If your house is for sale at $200,000 and a buyer asks if you will accept $185,000 almost any response you give can cause trouble. The right response is, "Let's put your offer in writing so we both know all the details. I actually have the blank forms for you right here." If you were to verbally accept the above offer at $185,000, not only does the buyer have no obligation to actually buy the house, many will say to themselves, "Hmmm....I wonder if $150,000 would work?"

WHAT ABOUT LOW OFFERS?

Low offers happen. Why? It may be the buyer's negotiation style, the buyer's finance limits or maybe the market has slipped since you began the selling process. No matter what the cause, do not take this personally. When you waste your energy being insulted, you are not investigating a great way to have that buyer be the proud new owner of your house.

All offers should be taken seriously. Either accept or counter-offer every offer. Treat every buyer with respect and in seriousness. If you do get a low offer, it is critical to get as much information as possible about why the low offer was written. Understand the motivation. Yes, it is your home and yes, you have put a great deal of love and effort into it, but taking a low offer as a personal affront serves no purpose and usually works against you.

RESPOND WITH YOUR INTELLIGENCE,
NOT WITH YOUR EGO

A nice house in a nice neighborhood belongs to a stubborn couple determined that since the neighbor's house sold for $200,000, by golly, their home should sell for the same price.

The Listing Agent told the couple their value topped at $188,000. He showed them the statistics. He showed them important differences between their home and the neighbor home. They stick to their price of $200,000 and after many months an offer arrives at $175,000. This Seller must stop thinking with their ego and work smart.

Accept Offer	Accept the offer as written with absolutely no changes.	MAY BE THE BEST DECISION!
Counter Offer	Counter-offer in the middle at $187,500.	WIN-WIN NEGOTIATION!
Reject Offer	Rejecting an offer can reject the buyer and the buyer goes away.	THE SCORE? SELLER ZERO, BUYER WON!

My Thoughts and Advice....

➢ The seller appears to be working hard to get along by meeting in the middle

➢ The buyer's agent will point out that the counter-offered price is absolutely in line with market value.

➢ The seller allows themselves and the buyer, pride. Pride is important in every negotiation. Most likely the buyer will accept this counter-offer.

➢ This counter-offer from the seller allows the buyer to come back with their highest and best offer.

➢ When you receive an offer that is close consider saying yes. Mitigate risk whenever possible in a real estate transaction.

➢ When the buyer wants to close early, say yes.

➢ When the buyer wants the table, the dog kennel and the house, say yes.

➢ When the buyer wants to buy for just a bit under full price, say yes.

Your must be flexible, analytical and accept the fact that every offer is written by someone who owns their own personality and style.

So what if the offer is low? So what if it is demanding? You have a buyer's signature and earnest money. This represents a serious buyer who is ready to buy. Your job is to analyze, understand, reason and turn the offer into a sale.

ACCEPTED OFFERS

Place your fully signed copy of the purchase and sale agreement in your file. Take a copy of the purchase and sale agreement to the escrow company. Make sure the finance company has a copy and that all inspections are ordered.

CLOSING CALENDAR	Deadline	Date Done	From /By	Phone
PSA Signed Mutual Acceptance				
PSA Delivered To Lender				
PSA Delivered To Title				
PSA Delivered To Escrow				
PSA Delivered To Buyer				
Financing Approval Letter				
Sale Of Buyer Home Contingency				
Inspection Contingency				
Insurance Contingency				
Feasibility Study Contingency				
Other Contingency				
Other Contingency				
Residential Disclosure Fully Signed				
Lead Based Paint Disc Signed				
Home Inspection				
Home Inspection Report Delivered				
Pest Inspection				
Pest Inspection Report Delivered				
Inspection:				
Inspection:				
Inspection:				
Closing Date Earliest				
Closing Date Latest				
Extension				

Real Estate, Real Advice
Exactly How To

Negotiate Smart

13

Everything is Negotiable
Negotiation Styles

EVERYTHING IS NEGOTIABLE

You may not like the fact that everything is negotiable but for the course of your home sale you need to live it.

WHAT IS NEGOTIABLE?

➢   Price.

➢   Financing.

➢   Contingencies.

➢   Dates: closing, contingency end dates, inspections.

➢   Who pays the costs of closing.

➢   Occupancy: When the Seller must move out and the Buyer may move in.

➢   Painting or repairs: Will the seller repair the roof, plumbing, windows, etc. and what style and quality of repairs will be made?

➢   Will the seller allow the buyer to perform repairs prior to closing? What are the risks?

➢   Fixtures: The standard rule is that any fixture attached to the house stays. If you choose to keep a certain light or other fixture in the house you are selling, then remove the item you want and replace it before you place the house on the market.

> Wall coverings: Do window treatments stay with the house or go with the seller?   (Read the fine print!)

> Furniture: Will the seller include specified pieces of furniture with the house? Any personal property that is included on the PSA will create an extra charge for sales tax.

> Buyers frequently request the seller pay buyer costs at closing. This usually becomes a tax deduction for the seller and actually allows the buyer to purchase without having much cash for a down payment. This is really OK. Make sure you calculate the extra expenses that a higher selling price causes and increase your selling price to cover buyer closing costs and increases in real estate commission, excise tax, title insurance, escrow fees, sales tax, etc.

> Nearly anything else.

> Negotiation gives you incredible power to create a favorable transaction. It can also place you in a position of immense weakness. The more knowledge you have, the better negotiator you will be.

WHEN THE BUYER MOVES QUICKLY

If there are stress factors, find out what they are. Knowledge is power. If you, as the seller are the one in stress, make sure you remain in the power chair by using the truth to your best advantage. The buyer is not the enemy. Talk to them! Find out what they are thinking. If you can get them talking, most people say too much and as a good listener, you will benefit.

In every negotiation each party sizes up the other. Find out why the buyer wants to buy now. Some reasons put more pressure on the buyer than others.

➢ Job transfer

➢ Signed contract to sell their current home

➢ Sold their current home and now living with extended family

➢ A baby on the way or Mom and Dad moving in

➢ A new job starting very soon

➢ A nearing date for the beginning of the school year

➢ The buyer's rental has been sold with a hard eviction date. They must move quickly!

MEN
WOMEN
AGENTS
BANKERS
BUYERS AND SELLERS
CAN ALL BE BULLIES

You may end up negotiating with a bully. Prepare yourself to calmly deal with all types of attitude. Think about everything you do from the other side's point of view. Only when you fully understand the other side can you do the best job of negotiating a winning transaction.

A bully's only power is in your reaction.

My Dad, a fully liberated chauvinist, recently said to me, "Professional women are bullies.

At a young age boys act like bullies and they get punched in the mouth.

Most girls, on the other hand, have never had the blessing of that particular real life lesson.

When we get away with bad behavior, we humans are likely to repeat it."

He may not be "politically correct" but I think he may be right.

Rather than reacting to any inappropriate behavior of your buyer, deal with them in a straight forward manner. Watch their face and their body language. You will quickly see the difference between what is truly important to them and what they say is important.

GOOD GUY
BAD GUY

This occurs when time is desired before making a decision or someone attempts to sway the direction of the sale. One person in the team is the good guy; the other is the bad guy.

Some teams create their plan to not be in the same room at the same time so they create an emotional roller coaster for the other side. The result is that rather than sticking to your plan, you tend to respond to what the Good Guy or the Bad Guy wants.

Solution: Make sure all parties are always in the room together. If you are working with a buyer agent insist that the buyer attend the negotiation. If there is no agent, meet with the buyers at a time when all decision makers are there. Get signatures on all paperwork as soon as possible.

NICKEL AND DIME

"We can't go any higher because we're short on down payment and closing money," or "We can not afford a higher payment."

Solution: This is a situation that tends to aggravate sellers. "Why are they making an offer if they can not afford this house", sellers ask me with a sense of deep insult.

As the seller, it's not necessarily price but net proceeds that you should focus on. Some lower-price sales can actually put more money in your pocket than a higher offer that asks you to pay heavy closing costs. Make sure you understand and work with the estimated settlement statement. The bottom line is that you need to stop caring about your sense a appropriateness. If you can help the buyer afford to buy your house, do it. You are successful when your house is sold.

NIBBLING AND WHITTLING

This technique is generally used after all agreements have been made and documents signed. The buyer might tell the seller, "I am sure you said the microwave was included in the purchase. Otherwise, I wouldn't have made a full-price offer."

Solution: Make sure everything is spelled out in the purchase and sale agreement and that no verbal offers or counteroffers are made. If one party starts nibbling at the other, remember adding items to the purchase and sale agreement can re-open negotiations. That often means loss, not gain, for the nibbler.

HIGHER AUTHORITY

This is when one of the parties must obtain decisions from another party who is not in attendance. The higher authority could be a spouse, an appraiser, a relative, even a boss. It's an easy way to stall for time while you evaluate all options before committing.

Solution: Set very short time frames for any offer that requires a response. You'll quickly learn if the higher authority is necessary in the decision making process.

THE STALL

The stall is a decision not to make a decision. It can mean that the buyer is not completely comfortable with this purchase or that there are some negative points they do not know how to address. It can also mean that the buyer is undecided between two properties.

Solution: Ask the stalling party to isolate their concerns about the offer. Go over each factor of the offer and discover the buyer's concerns. You now have a special strength you may choose to use. You can make sure the buyer is aware that you understand you can withdraw the offer any time before receiving signed acceptance. This may be the gentle push required for decision making.

ARE YOU FOR REAL

Make the negotiated item seem so insignificant the other party looks foolish saying no! For example, the buyer might say, "I won't pay the $5000 additional purchase price you countered back with." In other words, the buyer is willing to lose a house he loves and wants to buy over $5,000. (I have seen this happen over $2,000!)

Solution: Respond with, "The $5,000 additional will only cost you 47 cents more per day to buy this new home.   In monthly payments it is not much, but to me that $5,000 makes the difference of being able to sell or not."

LOGIC, REASON AND COMMON SENSE

Begin this tactic with a fairly priced house and a fair offer. Significantly overpricing houses runs off buyers. Making extremely low offers seriously irritates sellers.
Solution

> Pricing is always be based on comparable sales.

> Respect the other party's style, needs and behavior. When you know what is important to them you won't inadvertently push on their hot buttons.

> If you can not go down on price, consider paying some of the buyer's costs at closing or doing some of the needed house repairs yourself. This can increase your tax deductions so that your house sale results in the

same bottom line. Your costs to do the work may not be nearly what the buyer would pay a contractor.

➢ Be prepared to compromise.

➢ "Win-win" means that through the use of negotiation both buyer and seller win some, give some and end up in a good place for both.

➢ Approach negotiations from your top priorities and don't let your emotions overrule your judgment.

➢ Write down all agreements as they are made and then check off your list with the final purchase and sale agreement. If you don't get it in writing, it is probably not enforceable.

FIND THE MIDDLE GROUND

When there are simple disagreements over who will pay the recording fee, what date to use for closing or who will perform repairs, simply meet in the middle.   Pay half the fee. Do half the repairs. Meet in the middle between the buyers offered price and the seller's counter-offer. Splitting the difference is a time-honored successful negotiation strategy.

SET IT ASIDE

If you have a major sticking point that's not important to the overall contract such as the price of furniture being included in the sale, set that aside while you complete and sign the purchase and sale agreement. Solve minor issues in a separate agreement or amendment.

WHAT DOES THE MARKET SAY?

The housing market goes up and down. At different times we're in a "buyer's" market, a "sellers" market or a stable market where supply and demand are equal. You want to be in the market at a time when it favors _your_ position. Remember, all properties are unique. You can beat the trends, if your house appears special.

WHO HAS LEVERAGE?

If you're on the front page of your hometown newspaper because your business is bankrupt -- and the buyer knows it – the buyer is in the position of strength. On the other side of the table, if you have six buyers vying for your waterfront home, you now negotiate from the position of strength. Your job is to select the strongest buyer at the best price and terms for you.

In a multi-offer situation I frequently counter-offer back to every offer at the same time, giving each buyer the amount of the highest offer and requesting highest and best offer from each party.

This is fair and reasonable to every party as they have the opportunity to see ALL the facts and to show me who really wants the home the most. Even when all six come back with their highest and best offer you may choose a cash offer that is not the highest because it shows more strength and probability of actually closing.

DOLLARS ARE IN THE DETAILS

The price a sale is recorded at may include a number of extra expenses to the Seller. If you sell your house for $300,000 and agree to replace the roof before closing and you agree to pay up to $4000 in Buyer's costs at closing, then you did not really sell for full price.

You did, however increase your potential tax deductions and most importantly you got the house sold. If you look back at a sale where you made concessions and wonder if you gave away the farm, the answer is "You did perfect!" The house is sold, you have the money and your life is moving forward.

WHO WINS THE NEGOTIATION

In a transaction where one side has representation and the other does not, who has the advantage at the bargaining table? Do not assume that the representative is brilliant. The advantage goes to the:

➢ Most observant

➢ Best listener

➢ Most informed about the details of this transactions

➢ Most informed about the parties in this transaction

➢ Most adaptable person in the room

TERMS

A properly priced and presented home does not require much negotiation, but things will come up.

➢ Some buyers love to negotiate

➢ Some buyers want terms

➢ The offer may be contingent on sale of buyer's home

➢ Date of closing

➢ Lease purchase (a generally bad idea)

➢ Move in before closing (another generally bad idea)

- Store stuff in garage before closing (might be OK)

- Kick out renters before closing (high risk for Seller)

- Non-refundable earnest money

- Professional services needed such as repairs, title reports, feasibility studies

- Financing terms under which the buyer will perform on their purchase

- Inspections and who pays for them

NEGOTIATING TOOLS

- A smile

- Simplicity

- Strong listening skills

- A tablet and pen to put every detail in writing

- No agreement can be counted on until it is signed

Real Estate, Real Advice
Exactly How To

Get All

The Way to

Closed

14

Title Insurance
Escrow
Closing

Once you and a buyer have agreed on all the terms to your sale and signed the final copy of a PSA you will need a number of copies of that agreement.

➢ Seller

➢ Buyer

➢ Title Company

➢ Escrow Officer or Attorney

➢ Lender

Each of these people will perform a job that must be done to complete the transfer of the house to the buyer. The house will only be SOLD when it is CLOSED.

The sale of a home is CLOSED when the deed transferring title from the seller to the buyer is recorded by the county auditor. This is the actual time when the buyer owns the house.

Your house is FOR SALE until it is closed. Buyers die, get divorced, suffer auto accidents and get turned down for financing. Be <u>ready, willing and eager</u> to accept backup offers.

Maintain your beautifully staged house in showing ready shape during the entire process. You want the home as perfect for the appraiser as it was for buyers.

Place your PSA and all other documentation into a working file (ring binders are perfect) that you can take to negotiations, inspections, closing and other events. This file may be used for taxes and other reasons. Make sure you have:

➢ Listing Agreement (if listed)

➢ Buyer Agreement (if a listed buyer)

➢ Fully Executed Purchase and Sale Agreement with all addendums

➢ Copy of earnest money check and deposit receipt

➢ Preliminary Title Policy

➢ Closing Statement from Title Company

➢ Copy of Listing Feature Sheet

➢ All Other Back Up Documents

➢ Sellers Calendar

TITLE SEARCH

A title search is a thorough check of records concerning the property that is performed to verify the seller's right to change ownership. A title search uncovers demands, faults, liens and other privileges or restrictions on the property.

Carefully review the preliminary title report. It contains the exact legal description of the property and will tell you what liens and encumbrances are filed against the property. Review this document with your title officer.

WHAT IS TITLE INSURANCE?

Title insurance insures the new owner of ownership of the property. A basic policy insures the buyer is the owner and any lender shown on the policy is an "insured" lender. The title insurance policy fee is a one-time fee, paid at the close of escrow.

WHY YOU NEED TITLE INSURANCE?

Every parcel of land has a history. That history is tracked through ownership, sales prices and legal changes to the parcel.

Real estate may be the most valuable asset in your life. Title insurance assures you the property you are buying will be yours. Other than your mortgage holder, no one else should have any claims or restrictions against your home. Title insurance eliminates any risks and losses caused by faults in title from an event that occurred before you owned the property.

➢ It protects you, the insured, from a loss that may occur from matters or faults from the past.

➢ A title insurance policy will protect you from risks or undiscovered interests.

Bankruptcy, foreclosure, death, owner contracts, mortgage, liens, business ownership …. Many things can affect the transferability of your title. Know what is there.

Buyers commonly want to move in as soon as possible. When they learn there is a title problem that will take five months or more to fix, they often choose to move on to a different house. Luckily, this does not happen very often. If you check title first, it will not happen to you.

THE HIDDEN RISKS TITLE POLICIES PROTECT

- ➢ False impersonation of the true owner of the property by the seller or other persons previously in title

- ➢ Forged deeds, releases and other documents

- ➢ Deeds by persons of unsound mind

- ➢ Deeds by minors

- ➢ Invalid documents completed by an expired attorney

- ➢ Invalid deeds delivered after the death of the grantor

- ➢ Deeds by supposedly single persons but actually married

- ➢ Claims for unpaid estate inheritance and gift taxes against prior owners of your home

- ➢ Unrecorded easements – giving one party the right to enter another party's property

- ➢ Undisclosed descendents of former owners of your home or the land on which it is situated

ESCROW

An escrow is a deposit of funds, a deed or other instrument by one party for the delivery to another party upon completion of a particular condition or event.

The escrow officer will organize the requirements of the transaction and prepare documents for closing once the lending documents have been received.

EARNEST MONEY

When a purchase and sale agreement is written the buyer makes a deposit towards the purchase called earnest money. This money is normally held in escrow until the transaction is closed. At closing, the earnest money is credited toward the down payment.

The earnest money is typically protected for the buyer in the event the house does not pass inspections or the buyer's financing fails. These contingencies are written to protect the earnest money for the buyer for a specific length of time.

The purchase and sale agreement defines who gets the earnest money under each reason and timing the sale might fail. When the buyer fails to close without legal excuse, the earnest money goes to the seller.

Although it is rare for the earnest money to go to the seller I see an increased number of cases where the seller attempts to keep the earnest money. It seems the larger the earnest money the more likely there will be dispute. Please make sure you keep close track of all dates and agreement requirements.

WHAT TO DO WHILE IN ESCROW?

➢ Stay on top of every commitment, day, responsibility and person who is working on your transaction.

➢ Read the documents.

➢ Have the escrow officer explain the instructions from the other party and lender.

➢ The escrow officer will follow the written instructions given by buyer and seller in the PSA.

➢ React quickly to get all documents requested by your escrow officer. These may include a divorce decree, death certificate, manufactured home title or other documents.

➢ Respond quickly to correspondence. This will assist in the timely closing of the transaction.

➢ Request a copy of the documents and pre-read them prior to the scheduled signing appointment. Make notes of any questions.

➢ A cashier's check will be requested for all funds that are brought to closing.

GIVE BUYERS A FINAL WALK THROUGH

Is everything the way the buyer expects it to be? Have all the repairs been done? The buyer has a right to see that all work orders were properly completed and the house is in the same condition today, that it was in when they signed the purchase and sale agreement. This is a time when many sellers get insecure.

➢ Should I repaint the walls where you can see the outline of the pictures that hung on the wall. Answer: Was this a Top Dollar Sale? Yes. Use the paint that was left over last time you painted that room. Repaint the entire wall.

➢ Should I have the carpet cleaned? Answer: Yes.

➢ What should I do about the carpet stain that I forget to disclose? It was under a throw rug. Can I just leave the throw rug? Answer: No. If the stain can not be removed and it was not disclosed to the buyer in writing then you must talk to the buyer and find out if the stain matters to them. (They may be planning on new carpet!)

READ BEFORE YOU SIGN

Before closing you want to be certain that all the conditions of the purchase and sale agreement are met and that all directions given to the escrow officer have been performed. Before signing your name to any closing documents, check and double check that everything is correct.

Inform your closing agent that you will pick up all documents at least 24 hours prior to closing. If there is something you do not understand or agree with, get help.

➢ Take your transaction file with you to the closing table.

➢ Make sure the documents you sign at closing are an accurate documentation of your negotiation.

➢ If serious questions arise, obtain the necessary legal, accounting or other professional advice before allowing the documents to be recorded.

COSTS TO EXPECT AT CLOSING

Fees vary between companies. Each company will have a printed form of their standard fee schedule. On occasion, an additional fee will be charged for unusual expenditures of time on a given transaction.

The closing company has no control over the costs of other services that are obtained, such as the title insurance policy, the lender's charges, insurance and recording charges. Your closing officer can provide you with an estimate of the escrow fees and costs as well as fees charged by others, provided such information is available. Check with your attorney or closing company to assess the normal closing expenses in your area.

➢ Escrow and closing fees (includes sales tax)

➢ Title insurance (includes sales tax)

➢ Excise tax

➢ Real estate commission (f listing and/or buyer agent)

➢ Mortgage pay-off

➢ Home owners equity line of credit pay-off

➢ Liens of record

➢ Real estate taxes (up to the day of closing)

WHAT IS A CLOSING STATEMENT?

A closing statement is an accounting, in writing, prepared at the close of escrow which sets forth the charges and credits of your account. The items shown on the statement will reflect the purchase price, the funds deposited or credited to your account and payoffs on existing encumbrances.

The costs for all services and a determination of the funds you are entitled to at the close of the escrow are included.

When you receive your closing papers, review the closing statement. It is extremely logical and reflects the financial aspects of your transaction. If anything does not make sense to you, you should ask your escrow officer for an explanation.

When going through your final closing documents, examine all of them; there may even be a refund check hiding in there. Your closing statement and all other escrow papers should be kept virtually forever for income tax purposes. Your accountant will need the information about the sale or purchase of the property. IRS and other agencies may require you to prove your costs and/or profit on the sale of any property. The closing statement will assist in this task.

Do not rely on your escrow holder to retain the escrow file. Keep an organized file on every piece of real estate you own for tax and referral purposes.

WHEN YOU BRING MONEY TO CLOSING

All money brought to closing should be in the form of a cashier's check.

WHAT ABOUT CANCELLATIONS?

Cancellations happen. The purchase and sale agreement will define who is responsible for all closing costs or in the event the sale does not close, who pays the cancellation fees. These fees tend to be very reasonable.

The closing company will pay for all items that have been charged to the account, such as septic pumping, out of the earnest money if authorized to do so. The earnest money balance will be released to either the buyer or seller as dictated by terms of the purchase and sale agreement, but only after both parties have signed documents agreeing to the disbursement.

HOW OFTEN DOES A SALE FAIL?

I personally close 93% of the accepted offers I write. I have had agents work for me who closed only 50%.

The difference is in the Agent's (as a FSBO, you are your own agent!) willingness to be reasonable, thorough, a good counselor and have a common sense attitude when it comes to problem solving. Nearly every transaction has problems. If you are a problem solver, your odds will be similar to mine.

AT THE CLOSING TABLE

➢   Listen carefully

➢   Have all documents pre-read

➢   Do not be pressured

➢   Know what to expect

WHEN TO CLOSE

As Soon As Possible! Go out of your way, make a special effort, be inconvenienced with a smile on your face, just do what ever it takes to get closed as soon as possible. The longer you take to close, the more time you give disaster an opportunity to arrive.

WHAT IF THIS SALE FAILS?

Get another one.

AFTER THE SALE

➤ Send a quick thank you card to the professionals on the transaction and to the Buyer of your house.

➤ Make sure your name is removed from the utility accounts.

➤ Notify the paper boy of your new address.

➤ Send out change of address notification to your mailing list.

Every real estate transaction has risks and rewards.

Use this book to guide you past the risks, so you may reap the rewards.

ESTIMATED NET PROCEEDS AT CLOSING

Fill out for each offer to calculate the actual effect of all the terms.	
Selling Price	

Costs to be Deducted from Proceeds at Close of Escrow

Excise Tax	
Title Insurance	
Sales Tax on Title Insurance	
Escrow Fees	
Sales Tax on Escrow Fees	
Attorney Fees	
First Mortgage Payoff Balance	
First Mortgage Pre-Payment Penalty	
Second Mortgage Payoff Balance	
Second Mortgage Pre-Payment Penalty	
Real Estate Taxes Owed	
Water District Fees	
Irrigation District Fees	
Pest Inspection Fee	
Home Inspection Fee	
Septic Pumping and Inspection Fee	
Home Warranty Program	
Homeowner Association Fee	
Recording Fee	
Special Assessments	
Liens of Record	
Utility Closing Statements	
Seller Payment of Buyer Costs at Close of Escrow (Maximum typically 3%)	
Total of Costs to be Deducted	
Net to Seller at Close of Escrow	

REAL ESTATE, REAL ADVICE

Real estate is the largest asset you may own in your entire life.

With Real Estate, Real Advice you will learn to manage your real estate in the way that earns the security, comfort or wealth you desire.

ONLINE AT JULIDOTY.COM

- ➢ Real Estate Knowledge, Training, Free Articles
- ➢ The Secrets of Exactly How To Training Manuals
- ➢ Real Estate Tools
- ➢ Membership Listing Service with NO COMMISSIONS
- ➢ Training and Support
- ➢ Intensive Coaching Programs, Seminars, Workshops

www.JuliDoty.com or www.RealEsateRealAdvice.com

EXACTLY HOW TO SEMINARS

- ➢ For Sale By Owner
- ➢ Flipping Success for Real People
- ➢ Stage Your Home for a Top Dollar Sale
- ➢ Buy and Sell Real Estate Like a Pro
- ➢ Find and Manage Rentals
- ➢ Foreclosure, Divorce and Bankruptcy: All Sides
- ➢ Real Estate Agent Reality Camp

SPEAKER

- ➢ Weekly Radio Host
- ➢ Keynote Address
- ➢ Service Club and Senior Center Presentations
- ➢ Home and Garden Shows
- ➢ High Schools, Colleges,
- ➢ Radio and Television Programming

ON YOUR RADIO

When you want to know about anything real estate, Juli Doty tells it like it is. Real Estate, Real Advice is an innovative, honest and controversial show that answers your real estate questions on the air.

Juli Doty

REAL ESTATE HONESTY, REALITY AND FACTS

Every week Juli Doty gives direct answers to your real estate questions.

Home buyers and sellers learn the secrets of the real estate professionals. Flipping, staging, real estate methods and real estate rules become an open book as Juli Doty explains everything. Do you want to sell your home by owner? She will tell you exactly what to do. Remodeling, agents, or color selection, if it is about real estate, Juli Doty knows the facts and talks openly.

Listen every Saturday on a growing number of talk radio stations around the country. If your favorite station does not broadcast this show, call them and demand it!

CONTACT INFORMATION

Need "Real Advice" from Juli Doty?
advice@julidoty.com

Orders, Membership and Forms
service@julidoty.com

For Interviews and appearances
media@julidoty.com

Testimonials, Suggestions, Opinions
openline@julidoty.com

---

www.JuliDoty.com

JuliDoty.Com, Inc.
100 Malaga Highway
Post Office Box 4706
Wenatchee, WA 98807

(509) 662-7600
(509) 463-6311 Fax

Why did you initially buy this book? What did you find most useful? I appreciate your comments and suggestions.

_____

_____

_____

_____

_____

_____

Please add my name to your mailing list. I am interested in:

❏ Membership ❏ Information ❏ Seminars ❏ Newsletter

Send a free CD: Juli Doty live on Real Estate, Real Advice

Name _____

Address _____

City, State, Zip _____

Phone _____

eMail _____

Include my friend

Name _____

Address _____

City, State, Zip _____

Phone _____

eMail _____

JuliDoty.com, 100 Malaga Hwy, Wenatchee, WA 98801

Fax: 509.463-6311,
Online: www.JuliDoty.com

Abstract of Title

A compilation of recorded documents which relate to a parcel of land, from which an attorney or title officer may give an opinion as to the condition of title. This is also known in some states as a "preliminary title report."

Acknowledgment

A declaration made by a person signing a document before a notary public or other officer.

Adverse Possession

Most states have laws which permit someone to claim ownership of property which is occupied by him for a number of years. This is common where a fence is erected over a boundary line (called an "encroachment") without the objection of the rightful owner. After a number of years, the person who erected the fence may be able to commence a court proceeding to declare that the property belongs to him.

All-Inclusive Deed of Trust

See "Wraparound Mortgage"

ALTA

American Land Title Association.

Amortize

To reduce a debt by regular payments of both principal and interest.

Appraised Value

The value of a property at a given time based on facts regarding the location, improvements, etc., of the property and surroundings.

ARM

An adjustable rate mortgage, that is, a loan whose interest rate may adjust over time depending on certain factors or a pre-determined formula.

Arrears

A payment made after it is due is in arrears. Interest is said to be paid in arrears since it is paid to the date of payment rather than in advance.

Assignment of Contract

A process by which a person sells, transfers and/or assigns his rights under an agreement. Often used in the context of the assignment of a purchase contract by a buyer or the assignment of a lease by a tenant.

Assumable Loan

A loan secured by a mortgage or deed of trust containing no "due-on-sale" provision. Most pre-1989 FHA loans and pre-1988 VA loans are assumable without qualification. Some newer loans may be assumed with the express permission of the note holder.

Assumption of Mortgage

Agreement, by a buyer, to assume the liability under an existing note, secured by a mortgage or deed of trust.

Balloon Mortgage

A note calling for periodic payments, which are insufficient to fully amortize the face amount of the note, prior to maturity, so that a principal sum known as a "Balloon" is due at maturity.

Basis

The financial interest one has in a property for tax purposes. Basis is adjusted down by depreciation and up by capital improvements.

Binder

A report issued by a title insurance company setting forth the condition of title and setting forth conditions, which, if satisfied, will cause a policy of title insurance to be issued. Also known as a "title commitment."

Buyer's Agent

A real estate broker or agent who represents the buyer's interests, although typically his fee is a split of the listing broker's commission. Also known as a "selling agent."

Capital Gain

Profit from the sale of a "capital" asset, such as real property. A long-term capital gain is a gain derived from property held more than 12 months. Long-term gains can be taxed at lower rates than short-term gains.

Chain of Title

The chronological order of conveyance of a parcel of land, from the original owner to the present owner.

Closing

The passing of a deed or mortgage, signifying the end of a sale or mortgage of real property. Also known in some areas as "passing papers" or "closing of escrow."

Cloud on Title

An uncertainty, doubt or claim against the rights of the owner of a property, such as a recorded purchase contract or option.

Commitment

A written promise to make or insure a loan for a specified amount and on specified items. Also used in the context of title insurance ("title commitment").

Community Property

In community property states (CA, LA, TX, WI, ID, AZ, NV, NM, WA), all property of husband and wife acquired after the marriage is presumed to belong to both, regardless of how it is titled.

Comparables

Properties used as comparisons to determine the value of a specified property.

Condominium

A structure of two or more units, the interior space of which are individually owned. The common areas are owned as tenants in common by the condominium owners. Ownership is restricted by a Condominium Owners Association.

Contingency

The dependence upon a stated event which must occur before a contract is binding. Used both in the context of a loan and a contract of sale.

Contract of Sale

A bilateral (two way) agreement wherein the seller agrees to sell and buyer agrees to buy a certain parcel of land, usually with improvements. Also used to reference to an installment land contract (see below).

Contract for Deed

See "Installment Land Contract"

Closing Cost

Expenses incurred in the closing of a real estate or mortgage transaction. Most fees are associated with the buyer or borrower's loan.

Conventional Mortgage

A loan neither insured by the FHA nor guaranteed by the VA.

Cooperative Apartment

A cooperative is a corporation which holds title to the land and building. Each coop owner has shares of stock in the corporation which corresponds to an equivalent proprietary lease of his apartment space. Coops were very popular in New York City at one time, but are less common because of their lack of marketability due to high association fees.

Deficiency

The difference between the amount owed to a note holder and the proceeds received from a foreclosure sale. The lender may, in some states, obtain a "deficiency judgment" against the borrower for the difference.

Depreciation

Decrease in value to real property improvements caused by deterioration or obsolescence.

Documentary Tax Stamps

Stamps, affixed to a deed, showing the amount of transfer tax. Some states simply charge the transfer tax without affixing stamps. Also known as "doc stamps."

Double Closing

A closing wherein a property is bought and then sold simultaneously. Also called "double escrow" and "flipping."

Due-on-Sale Clause

A provision in a mortgage or deed of trust that gives the lender the option to require payment in full of the indebtedness upon transfer of title to the property (or any interest therein).

Easement

An interest which one has in the land of another. May be created by grant, reservation, agreement, prescription or necessary implication.

Eminent Domain

A constitutional right for a governmental authority to acquire private property for public use by condemnation and the payment of just compensation.

Encroachment

Construction or imposition of a structure onto the property of another.

Encumbrance

A claim, lien or charge against real property.

Equity

The difference between the market value of the property and the homeowner's mortgage debt.

Equitable Title

The interest of the purchase under an installment land contract (see below).

Escrow

Delivery of a deed by a grantor to a third party for delivery to the grantee upon the happening of a contingent event.

Escrow Payment

That portion of a borrower's monthly payment held in trust by the lender to pay for taxes mortgage insurance, hazard insurance, lease payments and other items as they become due. Also know as "impounds."

Estate

From the English feudal system, this defines the extent of one's ownership in a property.

Estate for Years

An estate limited to a term of years. An estate for years is commonly called a "lease." Upon the expiration of the estate for years, the property reverts back to the former owner.

Fee Simple

The highest form of ownership. An estate under which the owner is entitled to unrestricted powers to dispose of the property and which can be left by will or inherited. Also known as "Fee" or "Fee Simple Absolute."

Federal Housing Administration (FHA)

A federal agency which insures first mortgages, enabling lenders to loan a very high percentage of the sale price.

Federal Home Loan Mortgage Corporation (FHLMC)

A federal agency, commonly referred to as **Freddie Mac,** which purchases first mortgages, both conventional and federally insured, from members of the Federal Reserve System and the Federal Home Loan Bank System.

Foreclosure

A proceeding to extinguish all rights, title and interest of the owner(s) of property in order to sell the property to satisfy a lien against it. About half of the states use a "mortgage foreclosure," which is a lawsuit in court. About half use a "power of sale" proceeding which is dictated by a deed of trust and is usually less time-consuming.

Government National Mortgage Association. (GNMA)

A federal association, commonly referred to as **Ginnie Mac,** working with the Federal Housing Administration which offers special assistance in obtaining mortgages and purchases mortgages in a secondary capacity.

Good Faith Estimate

A lender's estimate of closing costs and monthly payment required by R.E.S.P.A.

Grant Deed

A deed commonly used in California to convey title. By law, a grant deed gives certain warranties of title.

Grantor/Grantee Index

The most common document recording indexing system is by grantor (the person conveying an interest, usually the seller or mortgagor) and grantee (the person receiving an interest, usually the buyer or mortgagee). All documents conveying property or an interest therein (deed, mortgage, lease, easement, etc.) are recorded by the grantor's last name in the grantor index. The same transaction is cross-indexed by the grantee's last name in the grantee index.

Heirs and Assigns

Words usually found in a contract or deed which indicate that the obligations assumed or interest granted or binding upon or insure to benefit the heirs or assigns of the party.

Homeowner's Association

An association of people who own homes in a given area for the purpose of improving or maintaining the quality of the area. Also used in the context of a condominium association.

Impound Account

Account held by a lender for payment of taxes, insurance or other payments. Also known as an "escrow" account.

Index

The measure of interest rate changes that the lender uses to decide how the interest rate on an ARM (adjustable rate mortgage) will change over time.

Installment Land Contract

The ILC is an agreement wherein the buyer makes payments in a manner similar to a mortgage. The buyer has "equitable title." However, the seller holds legal title to the property until the contract is paid off. The buyer has equitable title and, for all intents and purposes, is the owner of the property. Also known as a "contract for deed" or "contract of sale."

Installment Sale

A sale which involves the seller receiving payments over time. The Internal Revenue Code contains specific definitions and promulgates specific rules concerning installment sales and tax treatment of them. Also known as an "owner carry" sale.

Insured Mortgage

A mortgage insured against loss to the mortgagee in the event of default and failure of the mortgaged property to satisfy the balance owing plus costs of foreclosure.

Interest Rate

The percentage of an amount of money which is paid for it's use for a specified time.

Joint and Several Liability

A liability which allows a creditor to collect against any one of the debtors for the entire amount of the debt, regardless of fault or culpability. Most mortgage notes that are signed by husband and wife create joint and several liability.

Joint Tenancy

An undivided interest in property, taken by two or more joint tenants. The interests must be equal, accruing under the same conveyance and beginning at the same time. Upon death of a joint tenant the interest passes to the surviving joint tenants, rather than to the heirs of the deceased.

Judgment

The decision of a court of law. Money judgments, when recorded, become a lien on real property of the defendant.

Land Lease

Owners of property will sometimes give long-term leases of land up to 99 years. A lease of more than 99 years is considered a transfer of fee simple. Land leases are commonly used to build banks, car lots and shopping malls.

Land Trust

A revocable, living trust primarily used to hold title to real estate for privacy and anonymity. Also known as an "Illinois Land Trust" or "Nominee Trust." The land trustee is a nominal title holder, with the beneficiaries having the exclusive right to direct and control the actions of the trustee.

Lease/Option

An agreement by which the lessee (tenant) has the unilateral option to purchase the leased premises from the lessor (landlord). Some lease/option agreements provide for a portion of the rent to be applied towards the purchase price. The price may be fixed at the beginning of the agreement or be determined by another formula, such as an appraisal at a later time. Also referred to as a "lease/purchase."

Lease/Purchase

Often used interchangeably with the expression "lease/option," but technically means a lease in conjunction with a bilateral purchase agreement. Often used by real estate agents to mean a purchase agreement whereby the tenant takes possession prior to close of escrow.

Lien

An encumbrance against property for money, either voluntary (e.g., mortgage), involuntary (e.g. judgment) or by operation of law (e.g. property tax lien).

Life Estate

An estate in real property for the life of a living person. The estate then reverts back to the grantor or to a third party.

Lis Pendens

A legal notice recorded to show pending litigation relating to real property and giving notice that anyone acquiring an interest in said property, subsequent to the date of the notice, may be bound by the outcome of the litigation. Often filed prior to a mortgage foreclosure proceeding.

License

An authority to do a particular act or series of acts upon the land of another without possessing any estate or interest therein (e.g., a ski lift ticket). A license is similar to an easement in that it gives someone permission to go across your property for a specific purpose. An easement is a property interest, whereas a license is a contractual right.

Liquidated Damages

A contract clause which limits a party to a certain sum, in lieu of actual damages. In the case of a real estate purchase and sale contract, the seller's legal remedy is limited to the buyer's earnest money deposit.

Loan-to-Value Ratio

The ratio of the mortgage loan amount to the properties appraised value (or the selling price, whichever is less).

Market Analysis

A report estimating the resale value of a property.   Usually prepared by a real estate agent showing comparable sales of properties in the vicinity based on tax records and information from the Multiple Listing Service.

Marketable Title

Title which can be readily marketed to a reasonably prudent purchaser aware of the facts and their legal meaning concerning liens and encumbrances.

Mechanics Lien

A lien created by state law for the purpose of securing priority of payment for the price of value of work performed and materials furnished in construction or repair of improvements to land and which is attached to the land as well as the improvements.

Mortgage Broker

One who, for a fee, brings together a borrower and lender and handles the necessary applications for the borrower to obtain a loan against real property by giving a mortgage or deed of trust as security.

Mortgage Guaranty Insurance Corporation (MGIC)

A private corporation which, for a fee, insures mortgage loans similar to FHA and VA insurance, although not insuring as great a percentage of the loan.

Mortgage

A security instrument given by a borrower to secure performance of payment under a note. The document is recorded in county land records, creating a lien (encumbrance) on the property. Also known as a "deed of trust" in some states. The borrower is also called a "mortgagor."

Mortgage Insurance

Insurance required for loans with a loan-to-value ratio above 80%. Also called "PMI," or "MIP."

Note

A written promise to repay a certain sum of money on specified terms. Also known as a "promissory note."

Option

The unilateral right to do something. For example, the right to renew a lease or purchase a property. The *optionee* is the holder of the option. The *optionor* is the grantor of the option. The optionor is bound by the option, but the optionee is not.

Origination Fee

A fee or charge for work involved in the evaluation, preparation and submission of a proposed mortgage loan. Usually about 1% of the loan amount.

Performance Mortgage

A mortgage or deed of trust given to secure performance of an obligation other than a promissory note.

Periodic Tenancy

An estate from week-to-week, month-to-month, etc. In the absence of a written agreement (or upon the expiration of a lease once payments are accepted), a periodic tenancy is created. Either party can terminate this type of arrangement by giving notice, usually equal to the amount of the period or as prescribed by state law.

Points

Fee paid by a borrower to obtain a loan. A point is one percent of the principal amount of the loan. The borrower may usually pay more points to reduce the interest rate of the loan.

Prorate

To divide in proportionate shares. Used in the context of a closing, at which property taxes, interest, rents and / or other items are adjusted in favor of the seller, buyer or lender.

Purchase Money Mortgage

A loan obtained in conjunction with the purchase of real estate.

Quiet Title Proceeding

A court action to establish or clear up uncertainty as to ownership of real property. Often required if a lien or "cloud" appears on a title that cannot be resolved.

Quit Claim Deed

A deed by which the grantor gives up any claim he may have in the property. Often used to clear up a cloud on title.

Real Estate

Land and anything permanently affixed to the land and those things attached to the buildings.

Recording

The act of publicly filing of documents, such as a deed or mortgage.

Recourse Note

A note under which the holder can look personally to the borrower for payment.

Redemption

The right, in some states, for an owner or lien holder to satisfy the indebtedness due on a mortgage in foreclosure after sale.

Refinancing

The repayment of a loan from the proceeds of a new loan using the same property as collateral.

Re-issue Rate

A discounted charge for a title insurance policy if a previous policy on the same property was issued within a specified period (usually three to five years).

Release

An instrument releasing a lien or encumbrance (e.g., mortgage) from a property.

RESPA (Real Estate Settlement Procedures Act)

A federal law requiring disclosure of certain costs in the sale of residential property which is to be financed by a federally insured lender.   Also requires that the lender provide a "good faith estimate" of closing costs prior to closing of the loan.

Second Mortgage

A loan secured by a mortgage or trust deed, which is junior to a first mortgage or deed of trust.

Secondary Mortgage Market

The buying and selling of first Mortgages and Deeds of Trust deeds by banks, insurance companies, government agencies and other mortgagees.

Security Instrument

A document under which collateral is pledged (e.g. mortgage).

Settlement Statement

A statement prepared by a closing agent (usually a title or escrow company) giving a complete breakdown of costs and charges involved in a real estate transaction. Required by RESPA on a form HUD-1.

Specific Performance

An action to compel the performance of a contract.

Sublet

To let part of one's estate in a lease. A subtenant is not in privity of contract with the landlord and neither can look to the other for performance of a lease agreement.

Subject-To

When transferring title to a property encumbered by a mortgage lien without paying off the debt or assuming the note, the buyer is taking title "subject to."

Subordination

The process by which a lien holder agrees to permit his lien to become junior or "subordinate" to another lien.

Tenancy in Common

With tenancy in common, each owner (called a "tenant") has an undivided interest in the possession of the property. Each tenant's interest is salable and transferable. Each tenant can convey his interest by deed, mortgage or by a will. Joint ownership is presumed Tenants in Common if nothing further is stated on the deed.

Tenancy by the Entirety

A form of ownership recognized in some states by which husband and wife each own the entire property. As with joint tenancy, in the event of death of one, the survivor owns the property without probate. In some states, tenancy by entirety protects the property from obligations of one spouse.

Title

Title is the *evidence* of ownership. In essence, title is more important than ownership because having proper title is *proof* of ownership. If you have a problem with your title, you will have trouble proving your ownership to sell or mortgage your property.

Title Insurance

An insurance policy which protects the insured (purchaser and/or lender) against loss arising from defects in title. A policy protecting the lender is called a "Loan Policy," whereas a policy protecting the purchaser is called an "Owner's Policy." Virtually all transactions involving a loan require title insurance.

Truth in Lending

Federal law requires, among other things, a disclosure of interest rate charges and other information about a loan.

Warranty Deed

A deed under which the seller makes a guarantee or warranty that title is marketable and will defend all claims against it.

Wraparound Mortgage

A mortgage that is subordinate to and incorporates the terms of an underlying mortgage. The mortgagor (borrower) makes payments to the mortgagee (lender) who then makes payments on an underlying mortgage.

Yield Spread Premium

A "kickback" from the lender to the mortgage broker for the additional profit made from marking up the loan interest rate.